Therapeutic Attachment Relationships

Therapeutic Attachment Relationships

Interaction Structures and the Processes of Therapeutic Change

Geoff Goodman

JASON ARONSON
Lanham • Boulder • New York • Toronto • Plymouth, UK

Published by Jason Aronson
An imprint of Rowman & Littlefield Publishers, Inc.
A wholly owned subsidiary of The Rowman & Littlefield Publishing Group, Inc.
4501 Forbes Boulevard, Suite 200, Lanham, Maryland 20706
http://www.rowmanlittlefield.com

Estover Road, Plymouth PL6 7PY, United Kingdom

Copyright © 2010 by Jason Aronson Publishers

All rights reserved. No part of this book may be reproduced in any form or by any electronic or mechanical means, including information storage and retrieval systems, without written permission from the publisher, except by a reviewer who may quote passages in a review.

British Library Cataloguing in Publication Information Available

Library of Congress Cataloging-in-Publication Data

Goodman, Geoff.
  Therapeutic attachment relationships : interaction structures and the processes of therapeutic change / Geoff Goodman.
    p. ; cm.
  Includes bibliographical references and index.
  ISBN 978-0-7657-0745-1 (cloth : alk. paper) — ISBN 978-0-7657-0747-5 (electronic)
  1. Psychotherapy. 2. Attachment behavior. 3. Psychotherapist and patient. I. Title.
  [DNLM: 1. Object Attachment. 2. Professional-Patient Relations. 3. Psychotherapy. WM 460.5.O2 G653t 2009]
  RC455.4.A84G66 2009
  616.89'14—dc22   2009035433

∞ ™ The paper used in this publication meets the minimum requirements of American National Standard for Information Sciences—Permanence of Paper for Printed Library Materials, ANSI/NISO Z39.48-1992.

Printed in the United States of America

In memory of
Evelyn Eleanor Fries Steele
1907–1983

A haven of safety and a signpost to freedom,
you walked alongside me on the hazardous path to adulthood

Contents

List of Figures ... ix

Acknowledgments ... xi

1 Introduction ... 1
2 Freud's Influence on the Therapeutic Encounter ... 7
3 An Attachment-Based Pathways Model Depicting the Psychology of Therapeutic Relationships ... 23
4 The Therapist's Secure Base Provision and the Patient's Underlying Attachment Needs ... 45
5 Assessing the Patient's Attachment to the Therapist: Three Empirical Approaches ... 69
6 Interaction Structures Formed by Therapist and Patient Secondary Attachment Strategies ... 91

Afterword ... 101

References ... 103

Author Index ... 119

Subject Index ... 125

About the Author ... 131

Figures

Figure 3.1 Pathways Model of Working Alliance, Patient's Attachment to Therapist, Therapist's Caregiving of Patient, and Transference-Countertransference Paradigms   39

Figure 6.1 Typology Presenting Four Interaction Structures Based on the Secondary Attachment Strategies of Therapist and Patient   93

Acknowledgments

When I set out to write my second book, I never imagined that I would end up publishing three new books in a year. I need to make several general acknowledgments related to the realization of this book. Valeda Dent, associate university librarian for research and instructional services at Rutgers University, reproduced in PowerPoint the two figures presented in this book; read the entire manuscript for comprehension as well as grammar, spelling, and punctuation; located and obtained reference materials; and obtained the copyright for the painting for the book cover. Other than me, no one was more dedicated to the realization of this book than she was. Valeda's fingerprints are all over this document. Now we can turn our attention to writing our wedding vows! I hope that process will not take quite as long.

Marcia Miller, chief librarian at Weill Cornell Medical College, is simply the best librarian in psychiatry and psychology I have ever worked with. Long ago, I lost count how many times Marcia went out of her way to locate a reference, suggest other references that she thought might be helpful to me, or simply show an interest in what I was writing about. I wish all of you had a librarian of this caliber at your disposal, because you would understand the depth of my gratitude if you did. Dustin Kahoud, my faithful research assistant, alphabetized the reference section, a massive undertaking that he accomplished with a smile. Ian Rugg undertook the arduous task of checking the text citations against the reference section. Sushma Meka alphabetized all the journal articles and book chapters I cited and neatly placed them into folders. The Psychodynamic Research Listserv cofounded by Mark Hilsenroth and Andrew Gerber has educated me about many of the issues tackled in this book. I thank Mark and Andrew for inviting me to join the listserv. Darryl Voorhees produced the high-resolution digital image of the painting for the book cover. Cristin O'Keefe Aptowicz of the Artists Rights Society assisted with the use of copyrighted art. Julie Kirsch and Jessica Bradfield provided steady editorial leadership at Jason Aronson. Patricia Stevenson, production editor, does Jason Aronson proud with her meticulous work, which makes me sound almost like a professional writer. Leonard Rosenbaum, who also worked with me on my first book in 2002, provided the skill and precision necessary to compile the author and subject indexes. And various patients served as incidental clinical illustrations, for which I am grateful.

On a personal note, I wish to thank Marshall Silverstein, my esteemed colleague and friend at Long Island University, for offering constant encouragement and support in all my academic endeavors. Marshall is a true friend. Celeste Schneider has recently become a collaborator on various research projects. I am grateful to have her in my corner as an astute researcher, therapist, and friend. Dr. Marvin Markowitz, my psychoanalyst for the past thirteen years, has helped me to transform my own internal world and attachment. A simple "thank you" is not enough for showing me how to carry my emotional burden. My dear Uncle Ed and Aunt Fran urged me to include them in my acknowledgments, and why not? Throughout the entire process, they supported me with regular e-mail messages asking me about the book's progress. Finally, I want to acknowledge my mother, Carol Steele Goodman, and my late father, George David Goodman, for making me who I am. Everything begins and ends with them.

Chapter One

Introduction

It remains the first aim of the treatment in attaching [the patient] to the treatment and to the person of the doctor. To ensure this, nothing need be done but to give him time. If one exhibits a serious interest in him, carefully clears away the resistances that crop up at the beginning and avoids making certain mistakes, [the patient] will of himself form such an attachment and link the doctor up with one of the imagos of the people by whom he was accustomed to be treated with affection.

Sigmund Freud, "On Beginning the Treatment (Further Recommendations on the Technique of Psycho-analysis I)"

[The therapist] is to provide the patient with a secure base from which he can explore the various unhappy and painful aspects of his life, past and present, many of which he finds difficult or perhaps impossible to think about and reconsider without a trusted companion to provide support, encouragement, sympathy, and, on occasion, guidance.

J. Bowlby, A Secure Base: Parent-Child Attachment and Healthy Human Development

In this book, I invite the reader to consider the attachment relationship as an often-overlooked specific factor that nevertheless plays a key role in all therapeutic processes. I explore the attachment relationship as an effective ingredient in all therapeutic change. Even in treatments such as cognitive-behavioral therapy (CBT), where the therapeutic relationship is not considered therapeutic, this relationship nevertheless exerts a powerful implicit influence (see Craighead, Sheets, Bjornsson, and Arnarson, 2005).

Sigmund Freud and John Bowlby, the two minds who have most shaped my thinking about the processes of change that take place in psychotherapy and psychoanalysis, appear to be expressing in the quotations at the beginning of this chapter a commonly shared point of view about the curative nature of human relationship. The seventy-five years that span these two quotations, however, have yielded what I believe to be dramatic changes in the ways in which we conceptualize human relationship as curative. In fact, if these two men were able to sit down together in a pub in London to discuss the processes of therapeutic change, it is likely that they would find more differences than similarities in their positions.

These differences reflect changes in our culture, in the philosophy of science, and in contemporary views of human subjectivity. Heisenberg's uncertainty principle—the principle that the position of an electron cannot be determined because the observation of its position affects its position in an indeterminate way—has been appropriated as a metaphor for human interaction. Freud's foundational technical recommendations such as abstinence and neutrality have yielded to mutuality and subjectivity within the therapist-patient dyad. Attachment theory and research have begun to specify the variety of therapist-patient interactions and the relation between the quality of these interactions and patient outcomes. The goal of this book is to contribute to our understanding of these interactions and their influence on therapeutic changes in the patient.

I will now provide an overview of the chapters contained in this book. In chapter 2, I discuss Freud's influence on the therapeutic encounter and its limitations from an attachment perspective. I take the liberty of commenting on the quality of Freud's attachment relationship with his mother, his patient population, and his cultural context and the consequences of his particular technical and theoretical biases. I examine the evidence that supports my potentially controversial view that Freud's own attachment relationship with his mother was dismissing, or at least had dismissing features. This dismissing attachment relationship influenced Freud's technical recommendations for conducting psychoanalysis that instantly became the dogma followed by generations of psychoanalysts to come. I argue that these technical recommendations—namely, technical neutrality, abstinence, and management of the countertransference—might serve the needs of some patients, but other technical recommendations that assume a two-person psychology would be better suited for other patients.

In chapter 3, I explore an attachment-based pathways model depicting the psychology of therapeutic relationships. This model takes the caregiver-infant attachment relationship as a metaphor for the therapist-patient relationship. I address the advantages and disadvantages of using such a metaphor. How does the attachment relationship formed in earliest infancy inform our theory and conduct of the therapeutic relationship? How does this metaphor obscure us from examining other forces that shape the therapeutic relationship? I explore the differences between these two relationships—for example, the fact that care and attention are contingent upon a payment of a fee in the therapist-patient relationship. In spite of the differences, these two relationships are similar in the way in which the caregiver-therapist marks the infant-patient's affects as both experienced and understood by the caregiver-therapist and simultaneously not overwhelming to him or her. It is this containment of affects—carrying the emotional burdens of the patient without collapsing, retaliating, or avoiding them—that gradually moves the infant-patient toward development-health.

In chapter 4, I discuss the therapeutic principle of noncomplementarity—that dissimilar secondary attachment strategies in the therapist and patient produce more positive treatment outcomes than similar secondary attachment strategies (Dozier, 2003; Dozier and Bates, 2004). A therapist should be sufficiently secure and flexible in his or her attachment organization that he or she can challenge whatever strategy a patient presents with by adopting a noncomplementary strategy to provide a corrective emotional experience for the patient (Alexander and French, 1946). A therapist who tends to use a hyperactivating strategy must behave in a slightly deactivating manner with a hyperactivating patient to produce effective personality change. Conversely, a therapist who tends to use a deactivating strategy must behave in a slightly hyperactivating manner with a deactivating patient to produce effective personality change. Thus, the therapist provides a "gentle challenge" (Dozier and Bates, 2004, p. 174) to the patient's characteristic pattern of affect regulation and primary mode of relating.

In providing this gentle challenge to the patient, the therapist must behave as both an old, familiar object and a new, unfamiliar object. As a familiar object, the therapist provides the patient with the opportunity of developing various facets of the transference toward the therapist. The relationship to a familiar object often occurs in the understanding phase of treatment (Kohut, 1984). As an unfamiliar object, the therapist provides the patient with the opportunity of developing new expectations of the therapist's behavior that differ from the expectations developed from the familiar object's past behavior. The relationship to an unfamiliar object often occurs in the explaining phase of treatment (Kohut, 1984). A therapist who behaves only like the old object deprives the patient of the opportunity to develop new expectations and new modes of regulating affects and relating to others, while a therapist who behaves only like a new object deprives the patient of the opportunity of working through his or her relationship to the old object. I close chapter 4 with a clinical illustration of a five-year-old boy in foster care I treated in my private practice.

In chapter 5, I review three empirical approaches to assessing the patient's attachment relationship to the therapist: (1) the Client Attachment to Therapist Scale (CATS; Mallinckrodt, Gantt, and Coble, 1995; Mallinckrodt, King, and Coble, 1998; Mallinckrodt, Porter, and Kivlighan, 2005), (2) the Components of Attachment Questionnaire (CAQ; Parish and Eagle, 2003), and (3) the Patient-Therapist Adult Attachment Interview (PT-AAI; Diamond, Clarkin, et al., 2003; Diamond, Stovall-McClough, Clarkin, and Levy, 2003). Unfortunately, two of these approaches rely on self-report questionnaires that might be assessing defensiveness *against* the internal working model of this therapeutic attachment relationship rather than the model itself—its unconscious and conscious aspects. How does this research contribute to our understanding of the nature of therapist-patient interaction and patient outcome?

Patterned after the AAI (the gold standard for measuring adult attachment), the PT-AAI in contrast relies on narrative data to assess the therapeutic attachment relationship. Interestingly, the authors administered the PT-AAI to therapists as well as patients. The authors found that a therapist's RF coded from the narrative about the therapeutic attachment relationship differs between patients (Diamond, Stovall-McClough, et al., 2003). Thus, RF is not static or trait-like, but rather fluid and context-dependent—a process co-constructed by the two participants. I suggest that countertransference reactions can interfere with RF or even enhance it. I reanalyzed the authors' data and found that therapists seem to arm themselves with high RF when the patient has a history of unresolved, traumatic attachment experiences. Therapists seem to know instinctively when they need to understand the mental states of themselves and their patients to find their way in the midst of confusion fed by their patients' traumatic experiences.

Chapter 6 broadly outlines my thoughts about four potential interaction structures that therapist-patient dyads can form. I present a model for understanding how interaction structures develop out of the secondary attachment strategies of both members of the therapeutic dyad. Specifically, I propose a 2 × 2 typology in which the therapist's and the patient's secondary attachment strategies—deactivating and hyperactivating—form either complementary or noncomplementary interaction structures. I label the four interaction structures "sterile," "chaotic," "expressive," and "containing." I hypothesize that these four interaction structures are associated with four different treatment outcomes. Psychotherapy process researchers could empirically test this hypothesis by assessing therapeutic dyads for their attachment histories and observing the psychotherapy processes and outcomes that ensue. This four-category typology is not designed to capture the entire universe of relationships between therapists and patients, but rather to underscore four broad interaction structures based on what attachment-based psychotherapy research in its infancy is beginning to reveal to us.

This book is a sequel to my recently published two-volume work, *Transforming the Internal World and Attachment* (2009). In that work, I suggest moving beyond examining common factors such as the therapeutic alliance (Wampold, 2001) and turning our collective attention to common factors that psychotherapy researchers often erroneously promote as specific factors. I offer tentative ideas about other so-called specific factors that could function as common factors across all psychological treatments. In volume I, *Theoretical and Empirical Perspectives*, I review and discuss three theories about what makes psychotherapy effective across forms of treatment, treatment settings, and diagnostic categories: mindfulness, mentalization, and psychological mindedness. In volume II, *Clinical Applications*, I discuss the application of processes of therapeutic change from both psychodynamic and attachment perspectives. I close volume II with a most unusual application of therapeutic processes to four clinical interviews I conducted with two political refugees.

Therapeutic Attachment Relationships: Interaction Structures and the Processes of Therapeutic Change comes at a time when psychodynamically oriented therapists are becoming acquainted with attachment theory and the ambitious project to ground psychoanalytic theory and practice in empirical research and neuroscience findings. These ideas are just beginning to find publication in the psychoanalytic journals. No book has formally introduced the psychoanalytic audience to empirically derived processes of therapeutic change (e.g., therapeutic attachment relationships, interaction structures) within a theoretical framework grounded in psychoanalytic and attachment theories. The twofold shift to a two-person psychology and an empirical assessment of clinical evidence has created fertile ground for the psychoanalytic community to examine the compelling evidence provided by attachment research to support key aspects of not only its theories of development and psychopathology (Goodman, 2002) but also its processes of therapeutic change.

It has been twenty-one years since I walked into my first psychoanalyst's office for the first time and heard the words, "Are you in pain?" To understand the pain of another person, we must be open to experiencing that pain—in all its sadness, rage, desperation, and ultimately helplessness. This book attempts to understand the process of bearing the burden of pain in our patients and in ourselves in the therapeutic encounter.

Chapter Two

Freud's Influence on the Therapeutic Encounter

> A patient with whom I have been negotiating, a "goldfish," has just announced herself—I do not know whether to decline or accept. My mood also depends very strongly on my earnings. Money is laughing gas for me. ... The goldfish ... has been caught, but will still enjoy half her freedom until the end of October because she is remaining in the country.
>
> Sigmund Freud, "Screen Memories"

Freud devoted most of his writing to the unconscious motivational processes and defensive processes that comprise the human mind as revealed to him through psychoanalysis. He spent comparatively little time, however, articulating and refining the climate he cultivated in psychoanalysis with his patients. In fact, the majority of his papers on technique were written in a relatively short time span between 1910 and 1915, before he moved from the topographic model of the mind to the structural model of the mind (Freud, 1923). It is not clear whether Freud adjusted his technique to accommodate these theoretical changes or whether he believed that his technique worked equally well with both models. Similarly, his elevation of aggression to the position of a primary drive, equal in importance to sexuality, did not prompt him—at least publicly—to consider any technical adjustments to accommodate this new understanding (Freud, 1920). Thus, we have only the papers published from 1910 to 1915 on which to base our assumptions about the way Freud worked.

We know that Freud did not always follow his own recommendations, such as when he fed the Rat Man (Freud, 1909). Samuel Lipton (1977) has explained how ego psychologists reified Freud's technical recommendations to a point where they became a caricature of practice and an obstacle to treatment. It is not my intention to set up a straw man and criticize Freud's technical conduct (we do not have verbatim session recordings), but rather to examine his published technical recommendations and explore their intrapsychic, professional, and cultural origins.

Freud (1912b) presented to his colleagues a representational model for conducting psychoanalysis:

> I cannot advise my colleagues too urgently to model themselves during psychoanalytic treatment on the surgeon, who puts aside all his feelings, even his human sympathy, and concentrates his mental forces on the single aim of performing the operation as skillfully as possible.... The justification for requiring this emotional coldness in the analyst is that it creates the most advantageous conditions for both parties: for the doctor a desirable protection for his own emotional life and for the patient the largest amount of help that we can give him today. (p. 115)

By Freud's own account, the therapist seems to be a technician who plies his or her trade without emotional investment. At other times, Freud (1915) applied a metaphor of the chemist to describe the therapist's handling of "highly explosive forces" that demand "much caution and conscientiousness" (p. 170). The emotional life of the therapist is to be protected because of the explosive nature of the interaction. Similarly, the therapist must keep countertransference "in check" (p. 164) or "overcome it" (Freud, 1910b, p. 145) altogether. One gets the impression that emotions are toxic fluids that can contaminate the therapist and the therapeutic process.

Given the nature of this representational model of psychotherapy, the two technical concepts Freud offered to carry out the model should come as no surprise: neutrality and abstinence. For Freud (1915), neutrality is equivalent to avoiding emotional interferences: "Letting oneself go a little way in tender feelings for the patient is not altogether without danger. In my opinion, therefore, we ought not to give up the neutrality towards the patient" (p. 164). Freud (1912b) used the metaphor of a mirror to explain the neutrality of the psychotherapist, who "should be opaque to his patients and, like a mirror, should show them nothing but what is shown to him" (p. 118). Freud (1915) also believed that treatment should be carried out in an atmosphere of abstinence, in which "the patient's need and longing should be allowed to persist in her" (p. 165). In a later paper, Freud (1919) takes this idea further: "Cruel though it may sound, we must see to it that the patient's suffering, to a degree that is in some way or other effective, does not come to an end prematurely" (p. 163). Freud was suggesting that the technical concept of abstinence limits the patient's gratification by the therapist, which will motivate the patient to continue the work of treatment to alleviate his or her symptoms.

These technical recommendations, of course, manifest themselves in a spatial arrangement in which the patient is lying on a couch with the analyst seated out of sight (Freud, 1913). The disembodied analyst becomes even more depersonalized and therefore less gratifying, and the psychoanalytic encounter presumably becomes more neutral and abstinent. Interestingly, Freud (1913) revealed a personal motive for maintaining this arrangement: "I cannot put up with being stared at by other people for eight hours a day (or more)" (p. 134).

Although Freud (1912b) seemed to be aware that his technical recommendations would require modification in less than ideal treatment settings such as mental institutions, he remained silent about treatment modifications for specific patients or types of patients. In his seminal paper, "On Beginning the Treatment," Freud (1913) seemed reluctant to provide what today we would call a manualized treatment for conducting psychotherapy because, like a chess match, "the infinite variety of moves which develop after the opening defy any such description" (p. 123). Thus, it is possible that Freud routinely modified these technical recommendations in his own work, such as feeding the Rat Man (Freud, 1909) or sitting with his waitress Katharina and analyzing her while on vacation (Freud, 1893). Publicly, however, Freud (1912b) warned all those who do not follow these technical recommendations: "[The psychotherapist] should be in no doubt about what he is doing and should know that his method is not that of true psychoanalysis" (p. 118). It seems clear that Freud expected that his followers would follow these technical recommendations as general guidelines for all psychoanalytic treatment.

Just as Freud made specific technical recommendations for conducting treatment, so too did he take specific theoretical positions on which themes are important to listen for in the patient's verbal content and what method of intervention was curative in psychoanalytic treatment. The Oedipus complex—the intrapsychic conflict produced by loving the opposite-sex parent and hating the rival same-sex parent who also loves the opposite-sex parent—is "the central phenomenon" (Freud, 1924, p. 173) of childhood. Thus, the focus of Freud's treatment was to alleviate the patient of this central conflict through interpreting the unconscious wishes associated with this love and hatred for the parents. Any other intervention, such as suggestion, "achieves nothing towards the uncovering of what is unconscious to the patient" (Freud, 1912b, p. 118).

Bowlby (1982) reminded us that Freud addressed the reality of the infant's intimate relationship with the mother only in the final ten years of his life, when he accorded it the psychological significance more congruent with contemporary standards. Notably, Freud (1905) did seem aware of the mother's influence early in his career: "A child sucking at his mother's breast has become the prototype of every relation of love. . . . She strokes him, kisses him, rocks him and quite clearly treats him as a substitute for a complete sexual object. . . . She is only fulfilling her task in teaching the child to love" (pp. 222, 223). Yet the insight he displayed in this passage did not produce any lasting imprint on his theoretical architecture. In fact, in his final decade, Freud (1931) admitted his oversight: "Everything in the phase of this first attachment to the mother seemed to me so difficult to grasp in analysis—so grey with age and shadowy and almost impossible to revivify—that it was as if it had succumbed to an especially inexorable repression" (p. 226). Perhaps the centrality of the Oedipus complex was borne as much out of his confusion about early relationship experiences as it was out of his free associations and those of his adult patients.

In this twenty-first century, we can look back at Freud's construction of psychoanalytic technique and ask how he got there. Pioneers have no one to guide them. Truly, Freud made it up as he went along. In the absence of any historical landmarks, we could speculate about the personal influences on Freud's technical recommendations and theoretical biases. Hardin (1987, 1988a, 1988b) has written a trilogy of penetrating papers on Freud's relationship with his mother and nursemaid that bear on these issues. Although Hardin used these papers to argue for the importance of surrogate caregivers to our emotional development, we can underscore the insights gained by his work to develop an understanding of the nature of Freud's relationship with his mother. Then we will be in a better position to draw a connection between this relationship and his theory and technique.

Based on the available evidence, it appears that Freud developed what an attachment researcher might characterize as either a dismissing attachment relationship with his mother, or at least a secure attachment relationship with dismissing features. Quantitatively speaking (Kobak, Cole, Ferenz-Gillies, Fleming, and Gamble, 1993), Freud's primary attachment strategy might have been secure, but his secondary attachment strategy might have been on the deactivating end of the continuum. Of course, I am speculating because we know so little about Freud's early childhood. E. Jones (1953), however, provided valuable information, and Freud himself provided further clues in a letter to Wilhelm Fliess (Freud, 1897) and in his *The Psychopathology of Everyday Life* (Freud, 1901). E. Jones (1953) reported that Freud's mother abdicated her role as primary caregiver of her son at the time of the death of Freud's younger brother Julius, when Julius was eight months old and Sigismund (his given name) twenty-three months old. A nursemaid, who had helped Freud's mother with caregiving responsibilities since the time of Freud's birth, became Freud's primary caregiver until the birth of Freud's younger sister Anna, when Sigismund was thirty-two months of age. Simultaneous with this birth, the nursemaid was convicted of stealing from the Freud household and sentenced to prison, at which time Freud's mother presumably resumed primary caregiving duties. Just four months later, the family moved out of town altogether.

It does not take a psychoanalyst to sense the traumatic quality of these experiences for both the toddler Sigismund and his mother, who had her first son when she was only twenty years of age. When Sigismund was just fifteen months of age, his mother gave birth to Julius, who no doubt monopolized his mother's attention. The young Sigismund would have felt rejected and excluded from the care that his mother was now showing to this younger brother. We might expect a sense of hopefulness experienced by Freud at the death of his younger brother: *Now I can get my mother back.* Instead, Freud was relegated to the exclusive care of his nursemaid, a woman of questionable character who was stealing from the family. It is not clear why Freud's mother abdicated her role, but one suspects that she was overcome with grief over the loss of her second son. Perhaps to deny the loss, Freud's mother immediately became pregnant again and gave birth to another child nine months later. Sigismund no doubt noticed his mother's pregnancy and again felt rejected—another rival for his mother's love on the way. It seems plausible to assume that, given these circumstances, Freud began to depend on the nursemaid as an attachment figure. In a final series of crushing blows, the new baby was born, and, simultaneously, his attachment figure for the past nine months and caregiver for his entire life suddenly disappeared. As a toddler, Freud must have experienced the emotional and physical losses of his caregivers—both his mother and nursemaid—as a massive rejection of his own attachment needs. Caregiver rejection has been associated with the dismissing attachment pattern (Ainsworth, 1979; Ainsworth, Blehar, Waters, and Wall, 1978; Main and Goldwyn, 1984; Main and Stadtman, 1981).

Freud himself confirmed some of this speculation in both a letter to Wilhelm Fliess and in his published writing. Freud recalled a memory that occurred at the time of his sister's birth: "My mother was nowhere to be found: I was screaming my head off. My brother Philipp, 20 years older than me, was holding open a cupboard for me, and, when I found that my mother was not inside it either, I began crying still more, till, looking slim and beautiful, she came in by the door. . . . When I missed my mother, I had been afraid she had vanished from me just as the old woman [Freud's nursemaid] had a short time before" (Freud, 1897, p. 264). It seems that Freud was able to empathize with the feelings of a two-year-old, yet he labeled the story "amusing" (p. 264)—an obvious devaluation of his feelings of loss. In later years, Freud further dismissed the emotional import of this memory. After retelling the memory in *The Psychopathology of Everyday Life* (Freud, 1901), Freud added a telling footnote in 1924. The affect associated with this experience of loss, originally described in 1897 as profound anguish ("screaming" and "crying"), became "an affect of disappointment" (p. 51) by 1924, "derived ... from the superficial motivation for the child's demand" (p. 51). Freud was characterizing separation anxiety as a superficial motivation for his feelings, which he later characterized in this footnote as having to do with his sexual desire to have no rivals for his mother's sexual love.

A dismissing quality pervades the entire memory, from the minimized affect associated with it to its very interpretation. The sexualization of the memory could reflect an attempt to avoid the painful feelings of loss and rejection that such a memory elicited. This screen memory (Freud, 1899) also probably contains the traumatic affects associated with all the other losses occurring for Freud during that same period.

Still other clues suggest dismissing features of Freud's attachment relationship with his mother. Hardin (1988a) argued that Freud suffered profound alienation from his mother that lasted his entire life. From this alienation emerged a peculiar idealization of his mother that even infiltrated his theoretical writing. At age twenty-eight, writing to his fiancée, Freud praised his mother: "I do not know one action of hers in which she has followed her own moods or interests against the interests and happiness of one of her children" (E. L. Freud, L. Freud, and Grubrich-Simitis, 1978). Freud (1900) also reported a dream in which he saw "my beloved mother" (p. 583), toward whom he uncovered sexual desire. Years earlier, at age sixteen, Freud returned to his hometown of Freiberg and developed an admiration for the mother of a friend. Writing to his friend Silberstein, Freud made a comparison: "Other mothers—and why hide the fact that ours are among them; we shall not [love] them any the less for it—only look after the physical needs of their sons. Their spiritual development has been taken out of their hands" (Clark, 1980, p. 26). Freud seems to be reproaching his mother's perfunctory caregiving, but quickly extinguishes the reproach with an affirmation of love for her. The coding manual of the Adult Attachment Interview (AAI; George, Kaplan, and Main, 1996; Main and Goldwyn, 1994) describes this form of discourse as "positive wrap-up" in which a negative sentiment about a caregiver is quickly minimized by a positive sentiment. Such discourse is associated with a dismissing attachment pattern.

Freud (1912b) was aware that internal dynamics could pose a danger to theory building through the process of "projecting outwards some of the peculiarities of his own personality, which he has dimly perceived, into the field of science, as a theory having universal validity; he will bring the psychoanalytic method into discredit, and lead the inexperienced astray" (p.

117). In spite of this awareness, however, Freud was as vulnerable as any other theoretician to these dynamics. Surveying Freud's theoretical work, we notice a pattern of idealizing the mother-son relationship—"the most perfect, the most free from ambivalence of all human relationships" (Freud, 1933, p. 133). What happens to the man who is his mother's "undisputed darling"? "He retains throughout life the triumphant feeling, the confidence in success, which not seldom brings actual success along with it" (Freud, 1917, p. 156). These overgeneralizations are striking because they lack any sense of internal conflict or tension—a trademark of Freud's theory of the mind. Why is the mother-son relationship spared the *Sturm und Drang* characteristic of other object relationships? Freud wanted to believe in the security and wholeness of this relationship because he was defensively excluding painful childhood memories that portrayed a different relationship characterized by rejection and loss.

This defensive exclusion of psychological knowledge associated with Freud's relationship with his mother generalized to his understanding of female psychology. In 1926, Freud (1926) admitted, "The sexual life of adult women is a 'dark continent' for psychology" (p. 212). He could have just as easily substituted the word "me" for "psychology." E. Jones (1955) quoted Freud as having confided his confusion to his colleague Marie Bonaparte: "The great question that has never been answered and which I have not yet been able to answer, despite my 30 years of research into the feminine soul, is 'What does a woman want?'" (p. 468). We might wonder whether the latent version of this question was "What does my mother want from me to keep her from rejecting me?"

Further evidence for the dismissing features of Freud's attachment relationship with his mother comes from a survey of his reactions to his mother's death—a woman he consciously idealized. In a letter to his colleague Ernest Jones, Freud revealed what he characterized as a "curious" reaction to his mother's death: "An increase in personal freedom . . . and secondly, the satisfaction that at last she had achieved the deliverance for which she had earned a right after such a long life. No grief otherwise. . . . I was not at the funeral" (p. 152). The next day, Freud wrote a letter to his colleague Ferenczi, expressing a similar sentiment: "It has affected me in a peculiar way, this great event. No pain, no grief. . . . I did not go to the funeral" (E. L. Freud, 1960, p. 400). It is difficult to reconcile Freud's self-described curious reaction to his mother's death with a statement he made earlier in his career about the profound emotional significance of mothers: "A man|'s| . . . picture of his mother . . . has dominated his mind from his earliest childhood" (Freud, 1905, p. 228). All the evidence points to the conclusion that Freud's attachment relationship to his mother, whether secure or insecure, contained dismissing features. The historian Peter Gay (1998) suggested that Freud "was strenuously defending himself against the recognition that the tie to his mother was in any sense imperfect. . . . He seems to have dealt with the conflicts that his complicated feelings toward his mother generated by refusing to deal with them" (p. 506).

These dismissing features were not restricted to his relationship to his mother or to his theoretical musings about mother-son relationships. Victor Tausk, one of Freud's closest associates in the early days of his career, committed suicide. Freud wrote to his colleague Karl Abraham, "Tausk shot himself several days ago. You will recall his behavior at the Congress. . . . For all his significant talent he was useless to us" (cited in Gay, 1998, pp. 390, 391). In a letter to Ferenczi several days later, Freud wrote that he felt "no real sympathy" in himself over his friend's death "despite all appreciation of his gifts" (cited in Gay, 1998, p. 391). Freud's feelings over the loss of close relationships seem to be defensively excluded from his awareness.

According to the coding manual of the AAI, dismissing persons "limit the influence of attachment relationships and experiences in thought, in feeling, or in daily life" (Main and Goldwyn, 1994, p. 126). During the interview, dismissing persons provide little information about their childhoods and offer semantic memories of idealized caregivers combined with episodic memories of rejection; they usually score high on the rejection, idealization, lack of recall, and derogation scales. These persons deactivate attachment needs by "restricting access to attachment memories, idealizing parents, or devaluing attachment relationships" (Kobak et al., 1993, p. 233). Dismissing persons thus deny distress, limit their affective engagements with caregivers (Cassidy and Kobak, 1988), and become compulsively self-reliant (Bowlby, 1973). That Freud worked 13.5-hour days, six days a week (Freud, 1913, 1914), visited his mother out of obligation (Masson, 1985, p. 306), and conducted his own analysis by himself (Freud, 1900) further supports the image of a compulsively self-reliant man working in a profession many perceive as lonely (Greenson, 1967) but in no particular need of caregiving or help. The concept of attachment as a motivational system distinct and independent from libido remained undiscovered until Bowlby, perhaps because Freud tended to dismiss the emotional significance of attachments in his own life.

I am not suggesting that Freud would have necessarily been classified as dismissing had someone administered the AAI to him. Other fathers of clinical psychology would fit the coding guidelines for dismissing attachment more closely than Freud. John B. Watson, widely considered the father of behaviorism, displayed a decidedly dismissing attitude toward parenting: "Treat [children] as though they were young adults. . . . Let your behavior always be objective and kindly firm. Never hug and kiss them, never let them sit on your lap. If you must, kiss them once on the forehead when they say good night. Shake hands with them in the morning" (Watson, 1928, pp. 81, 82). The ideal child, according to Watson (1928), is "a child who never cries unless actually stuck by a pin . . . who puts on such habits of politeness and neatness and cleanliness that adults are willing to be around him at least part of the day" (p. 9). Any kind of secure-base behavior exhibited by a mother enraged him: "When I hear a mother say 'Bless its little heart' when it falls down, or stubs its toe, or suffers some other ill, I usually have to walk a block or two to let off steam" (Watson, 1928, p. 82). Outrageous as these words might sound, Watson went further, questioning "whether there should be individual homes for children—or even whether children should know their own parents. There are undoubtedly more scientific ways of bringing up children which probably mean finer and happier children" (Watson, 1928, pp. 5, 6). Even though Freud was not known to kiss his own children (Gay, 1998, p. 162), he seems like the paragon of a securely attached person by comparison.

Rather than definitively portraying Freud as dismissing of attachment, I am arguing that Freud's internal working model contained dismissing features that likely affected his technical recommendations and theoretical formulations. Just as there is some truth to the saying "You can tell a lot about a man by the shoes he wears," so too you can tell a lot about a theoretician by the theories he or she formulates. Watson formulated behaviorism, which postulated that only what is observable exists, and only behavior is observable. Where is the love in this theory? Where was the love in Watson? By contrast, Freud formulated a cure "effected by love" (Freud, 1906, p. 13). But perhaps the dismissing features associated with Freud's internal working model crept into his technical recommendations and theorizing. Freud's two technical concepts—neutrality and abstinence—as well as his recommendation to overcome countertransference, the exclusive use of the couch, and his virtual disregard of the importance of the mother-child relationship to development and psychopathology, could reflect "peculiarities of his own personality" that he projected "into the field of science, as a theory having universal validity" (Freud, 1912b, p. 117). Many years later, the field still struggles with Freud's theories and their application to the psychotherapeutic encounter.

It is important to keep in mind that Freud formulated his technical recommendations while working mostly with a population of patients diagnosed with hysteria. Attachment researchers (Bernier and Dozier, 2002; Bernier, Larose, and Soucy, 2005; Dozier, 2003; Dozier and Bates, 2004; Dozier, Cue, and Barnett, 1994; Dozier and Tyrrell, 1998; Tyrrell, Dozier, Teague, and Fallot, 1999) have begun to demonstrate that the most effective treatments pair a patient with one particular secondary attachment strategy (i.e., dismissing or preoccupied) with a therapist with the other strategy (see chapter

3). Thus, a treatment is particularly effective if the patient has preoccupied features, while the therapist has dismissing features, and vice versa. This is known as the therapeutic principle of noncomplementarity.

Studies of the therapist's attachment organization (Bernier and Dozier, 2002; Bernier et al., 2005; Dozier, 2003; Dozier and Bates, 2004; Dozier et al., 1994; Dozier and Tyrrell, 1998; Tyrrell et al., 1999) suggest that most therapists are securely attached yet nevertheless rely on a secondary attachment strategy when the first one falters. If we view these secondary attachment strategies as patterns of affect regulation that range on a continuum from dismissing to preoccupied, a 2 × 2 matrix is created between these two strategies in therapists and patients (see figure 6.1). According to Kobak and his colleagues (Kobak et al., 1993), dismissing features indicate a strategy of deactivating the attachment system by overregulating affect, while preoccupied features indicate a strategy of hyperactivating the attachment system by underregulating affect. Both strategies are designed to deactivate the attachment system. A person using the dismissing strategy seeks to deactivate the system on one's own, while a person using the preoccupied strategy seeks to deactivate the system by exaggerating affective displays to elicit deactivating behavior from someone else (e.g., caregiver or therapist; see also Goodman, 2002).

André Brouillet's famous 1887 painting of Jean-Martin Charcot presenting his pet hysteric "Blanche" (Blanche Wittman) to his fellow physicians visually captures the hysteric's signature exaggerated affective display, perhaps a marker of a hyperactivating attachment strategy. The current label of hysteria—histrionic personality disorder (American Psychiatric Association, 2000)—consists of additional criteria such as demands for reassurance, approval, or praise, sexually seductive behavior, and an excessively impressionistic style of speech—personality traits consistent with a hyperactivating attachment strategy. In fact, this style of speech is one of the hallmarks of a preoccupied attachment strategy documented in the AAI coding guidelines (Main and Goldwyn, 1994). If Freud's bread-and-butter patient was the hysteric (e.g., Freud, 1893–1895), and hysterics use preoccupied attachment strategies to deactivate their attachment systems, then it would be reasonable to conclude that many, if not most, of Freud's patients suffered from underregulated affect associated with a preoccupied attachment strategy. If Freud were intuitively aware of the principle of noncomplementarity, then the technical recommendations of neutrality, abstinence, and overcoming the countertransference could be reconceptualized as effective therapeutic tools *applied to this particular population*. It seems reasonable to suggest that Freud's (1906) cure "effected by love" (p. 13) required an overregulated therapeutic technique to contain the underregulated affect of his hysterical patients. In other words, Freud's apparent dismissing features and overregulated affect might have served him quite well, given the diagnostic and attachment features of his caseload.

We must also keep in mind that the cultural background at the time of Freud, situated in the sexually repressed and repressive Victorian era (Gay, 1998), could be considered an era in which a dismissing attachment strategy ruled and, in some regions of Germany, still rules. In a northern German sample, for example, attachment researchers (Grossmann, Grossmann, Spangler, Suess, and Unzner, 1985) found a disproportionately high percentage of infants classified as anxious-avoidant (the infant analogue of dismissing). The authors hypothesized that German parents' emphasis on independence and self-reliance contributed to this unexpected outcome. At the time of Freud, nannies routinely assumed primary caregiving duties in bourgeois society, which no doubt produced an epidemic of feelings of rejection and loss that forced children to rely on themselves to deactivate attachment needs and overregulate their affects. Freud's childhood history was probably not dramatically different from anyone else's growing up during that era. Thus, his technical recommendations and theoretical formulations, however quaint to us, are congruent with his personal childhood history, patient population, and cultural background.

Contemporary psychoanalysis, embodied particularly in relational psychoanalytic theory and attachment theory, recognizes the dialectic of technical recommendations: they must be distinctive enough to be applicable to more than one therapist-patient dyad but flexible enough to be applicable to the unique relationship created between each therapist and patient. Our field has often emphasized one of the poles of the dialectic to the exclusion of the other pole. As I have shown, Freud emphasized the universality of his technical recommendations. Freud's technical recommendations might have been effective with the population he was working with, but ineffective in other therapeutic contexts. One of the current champions of universal technical recommendations is Michels (2001), who acknowledged the pitfalls of adhering to "only one right way" (p. 409) of technique; however, according to him, "We do have preferred ways of working, and patients would be foolish to come to us if we did not" (p. 410).

On the other side of the spectrum, champions of the uniqueness of the therapeutic relationship created by the therapist and patient dismiss "preferred ways of working" and, at times, advocate "throwing away the book" (I. Z. Hoffman, 1994, p. 187). J. Greenberg (2001a), a proponent of maximum flexibility of technique, argued, "There is no way . . . to assert *a priori* the benefit of any technical intervention" (p. 364) because of the uniqueness of the therapeutic dyad and the inherent unpredictability of intervention effects.

Other writers (e.g., Kantrowitz, 2001) have expressed similar sentiments: "An analytic treatment is like a snowflake. Overall, it is easy to identify and distinguish. However, closer scrutiny reveals how different each one is from the others. In fact, no two are alike. Nor are any two patient-analyst pairs. In analytic treatment, the particular aspects of therapeutic action that facilitate psychological change are likely to vary from person to person" (p. 403). Therapists within a broad psychodynamic tradition can readily identify with these sentiments because the interaction structures (Jones, 2000) that develop in all our clinical work do feel unique within each therapeutic encounter we have. Yet most of us adhere to a set of technical guidelines that somehow remain constant across patients. J. Greenberg (2001b) suggested that this technical flexibility—the willingness to vary technique according to the nature of the patient's personality and psychopathology and the ever-changing therapeutic relationship—constitutes an advance in psychoanalytic clinical theory. The parameters of this variation, however, remain largely unspecified in the relational literature.

In a paper written during the infancy of relational theory, J. R. Greenberg (1986) suggested that technical taboos such as emotional openness, self-disclosure, and even judgment could be used judiciously in certain contexts within the psychotherapeutic encounter to further the treatment aims. For example, expressing surprise and concern at a patient's determined self-destructive behavior could present the patient with a caregiving experience that differs from the indifferent one they knew from childhood. From an object relations perspective, Kernberg and his colleagues (e.g., Kernberg et al., 1989) have considered this position as an extension of technical neutrality because any so-called normal person would have the same emotional reaction to this behavior, which is important for the patient to observe and internalize. Under these circumstances, "the traditionally neutral non-judgmental attitude," according to J. R. Greenberg (1986), "can be genuinely dangerous" (p. 146). Freud, then, by virtue of his fixed technical recommendations, could have been dangerous because, with certain patients, he was unwittingly repeating their childhood experiences with a neglectful parent.

J. R. Greenberg (1986) concluded that an effective treatment requires the patient to experience the therapist as both an old and a new object. In other words, a dialectic exists between the patient's experience of the therapist as an object of the patient's transference and the experience of the therapist as someone who behaves differently from the original objects from childhood. If, like Freud, the therapist adopts a fixed technique vis-à-vis the therapeutic relationship, technical errors in either direction could follow. In the first scenario, the therapist could be behaving too much like the parents of childhood. From an attachment perspective, this technical error comes in two forms:

therapists with dismissing features paired with patients with dismissing features, and therapists with preoccupied features paired with patients with preoccupied features (see figure 6.1). These pairings are less conducive to therapeutic change than noncomplementary pairings in which dismissing features are paired with preoccupied features (Bernier and Dozier, 2002; Bernier et al., 2005; Dozier, 2003; Dozier and Bates, 2004; Dozier et al., 1994; Dozier and Tyrrell, 1998; Tyrrell et al., 1999).

In the second scenario, the therapist could be behaving so differently from the parents of childhood that the transference is not permitted to emerge, and the therapy thus never gets under way (J. R. Greenberg, 1986). The attachment literature has not addressed the implications of this second scenario. Related to this scenario, Diamond and her colleagues (Diamond, Stovall-McClough, Clarkin, and Levy, 2003) have suggested that therapists' levels of mentalization must be neither too discrepant nor too parallel to their patients' levels of mentalization for changes in mentalization to occur (see chapter 5; see also Goodman, in press-a, chapter 6). In other words, the patient's development of the capacity to understand the mental states of self and others depends on the therapist's ability to titrate the patient's understanding by mentalizing at a level just above that of the patient—a concept similar to Vygotsky's (1978) zone of proximal development. Dozier and Bates (2004) also mentioned that the "gentle challenge" (p. 174) provided by the therapist's provision of an attachment experience noncomplementary to the patient's attachment pattern must occur within a trusting therapeutic relationship, which implies that a forceful challenge could disrupt the therapeutic alliance (Zetzel, 1956) and end the treatment. Perhaps what a patient needs for treatment to succeed is a therapist who permits the patient to behave toward him as though he were an old object, yet responds differently to the patient than the old object behaved (Casement, 2001). This idea integrates the patient's use of the therapist as a transference object with the therapist's noncomplementary response to this use. The "technique" of the therapist—to survive the negative transference without collapsing or retaliating (as the patient's caregivers had)—constitutes a therapeutically transforming experience (Casement, 2001).

Freud (1915) formulated his technical recommendations to maximize the opportunity for the patient to develop the transference. We have seen, however, that the technical concepts of neutrality, abstinence, and overcoming the countertransference fail to promote the perception of the therapist as a mirror because each patient experiences these conditions differently, depending on their expectations of caregiver behavior. These classical technical concepts instead create the conditions for perceiving the therapist as either like the deactivating, dismissing parents of childhood (e.g., abstinent and neglectful), or like a new object who responds differently from the hyperactivating, preoccupied parents of childhood (e.g., calm and reflective). I have argued that, following the principle of noncomplementarity, Freud's technical recommendations are better suited to patients with hyperactivating attachment strategies (like the hysterics he mostly treated) than to patients with deactivating attachment strategies. Relational theory and attachment theory and research suggest, however, that the therapist needs to be flexible and adjust his or her technique to accommodate the patient's pattern of affect regulation and thus create the treatment conditions that optimize the use of the therapeutic relationship. Specifically, the therapist must not only permit the transference to emerge but also respond to this transference in ways that gently challenge the patient's expectations formed during numerous interactions with the parents during childhood.

Clinical theoreticians and researchers alike have been attempting to enhance our understanding of the patient's mental representations of the therapist and the relationship to the therapist and their roles in therapeutic change. Treurniet (1993) suggested that therapeutic change takes place through the nonverbal interactions between therapist and patient as well as through the classical vehicles of insight and interpretation. Recently, Eagle (2003, p. 48) supported this view with a clinical vignette of a female patient who experienced the permanent remission of dyspareunia after an interaction with him that the two of them never discussed following the interaction. According to Eagle, he never made an interpretation of the interaction or the outcome.

Freud never acknowledged a therapeutic role for the nonverbal relationship between the therapist and the patient. Freud (1909) fed the Rat Man but never considered that behavior therapeutic. In fact, Freud (1919) considered the uncovering of repressed material through interpretation—"the pure gold of analysis"—superior to "the copper of direct suggestion" (p. 168) and other forms of psychotherapy such as hypnosis, which he had abandoned. He considered the nonverbal aspects of the therapeutic relationship, such as the use of the couch, only as conditions under which the patient's transference could manifest itself. The idea that the therapeutic relationship might have healing properties independent of interpretation received its first hearing with books by Ferenczi and Rank (1924) and Alexander and French (1946), the latter introducing the term "corrective emotional experience." This experience includes not only verbal but also nonverbal interactions between the therapist and patient. Dyadic interactions that do not rely on verbal meanings such as activity level, conversational engagement, prosodic emphasis, and vocal mirroring accounted for 30 percent of the outcome of the first five minutes of a simulated employment negotiation (Curhan and Pentland, 2007). Both therapist and patient monitor these alternative channels of communication to help formulate their mental image of the other person and the interactions between them.

In summary, I have attempted to demonstrate that Freud formulated his technical recommendations consistent with dismissing features of his attachment organization, hyperactivating patterns of affect regulation within his patient population, and cultural restrictions (which also reflect dismissing features of attachment within that culture). I argued that although Freud meant for therapists to apply these technical recommendations universally to all patients, their effectiveness is probably restricted to a subset of patients with preoccupied features of attachment. We will never know how psychoanalytic technique would have evolved had Freud's attachment strategy been less dismissing. Perhaps the outcome would have been a more relationally oriented clinical technique from the outset.

Relational theory and attachment theory and research have presented credible challenges to classical psychoanalytic technique. Theoreticians working within these perspectives are recommending a more flexible approach to clinical technique, anchored around the pattern of affect regulation presented by the patient, both within and across sessions. A tentative technical recommendation offered by this group and supported by preliminary evidence is to present a gentle challenge to the patient's preferred pattern of affect regulation that embodies their attachment strategy. This principle of noncomplementarity provides the broad technical conditions under which a corrective emotional experience can occur.

The target of therapeutic change has also begun to shift away from the verbalization of repressed unconscious material through interpretation to nonverbal channels of interaction. The study of these nonverbal channels operating between the therapist and patient depends on the metaphor of the caregiver-infant attachment relationship. In chapter 3, I examine the caregiver-infant attachment relationship as a metaphor for the therapist-patient relationship. As I have demonstrated, Freud did not use this metaphor to guide his thinking about the therapist-patient relationship. For the most part, Freud viewed the patient's relationship to the therapist as a pseudorelationship in which the patient transfers the childhood relationship with the caregivers onto the therapist. Consistent with this view, the therapist should conduct the treatment in abstinence. According to Freud (1915), "The patient's need and longing should be allowed to persist in her, in order that they may serve as forces impelling her to do work and to make changes" (p. 165). From this statement, we could surmise that the therapist's conduct resembles *anti*-caregiving; a caregiver does not permit an infant's need and longing to persist. In chapter 3, I explore the advantages and disadvantages of using this metaphor for the therapist-patient relationship.

Chapter Three

An Attachment-Based Pathways Model Depicting the Psychology of Therapeutic Relationships

> In providing his patient with a secure base from which to explore and express his thoughts and feelings the therapist's role is analogous to that of a mother who provides her child with a secure base from which to explore the world. The therapist strives to be reliable, attentive, and sympathetically responsive to his patient's explorations and, so far as he can, to see and feel the world through his patient's eyes, namely to be empathic.
>
> J. Bowlby, A Secure Base: Parent-Child Attachment and Healthy Human Development

Throughout the history of psychotherapy, clinical theoreticians have evoked various metaphors to depict the therapist-patient relationship. With the advent of attachment theory and other advances in developmental psychology in the 1950s and 1960s, a new therapeutic metaphor was born: the caregiver-infant attachment relationship. This metaphor has yielded a number of insights into the process of psychotherapy and the nature of the interactions in which the therapist and patient engage. The first objective of this chapter is to illuminate both the advantages and disadvantages of using this metaphor to depict the psychology of therapeutic relationships. One distinction between this metaphor and the therapeutic relationship is the state of development of mental structures in the infant versus the patient. Whereas the caregiver is behaving in response to the infant's emotional cues not contextualized by an interactional history of expectations to guide these cues, the patient enters into a therapeutic relationship with a complex and intricate interactional history of expectations. This asynchrony between the caregiver-infant attachment relationship and the therapist-patient relationship requires the therapist to behave in sometimes noncomplementary ways to challenge and interpret these transferential patterns rather than simply responding to emotional cues, as a caregiver would do. These interactional expectations, typically organized around definable patterns of behavior in the therapeutic relationship, are "often neither conscious and verbalizable nor repressed in the dynamic sense" (Lyons-Ruth, 1999, p. 589), and thus pose challenges to traditional psychotherapy models that rely exclusively on symbolization to produce therapeutic change. This new understanding of therapeutic change forces therapists to focus more intensively on their own attitudes and behaviors vis-à-vis the patient as the quintessential instruments of change. Various aspects of the therapeutic relationship, in addition to verbalized interpretations of repressed conflict, have thus come under increased scrutiny. I present an attachment-based pathways model for understanding the interrelations among three relationship-based concepts used in contemporary psychotherapies: working alliance, patient attachment and therapist caregiving, and transference and countertransference. Thus, the second objective of this chapter is to sensitize therapists and psychotherapy process researchers to the structure and functioning of these interrelated concepts to increase therapeutic effectiveness.

Each of us carries with us into our therapy office a metaphor—conscious and unconscious—of our relationship with our patients. This metaphor varies from patient to patient, and varies within the same patient across the span of treatment. Nevertheless, the broad parameters of this metaphor probably remain constant, both within and across patients, and depend on the quality of our own attachment patterns and broader influences. Each theoretical perspective also inaugurates and sanctions its own ready-made therapeutic metaphors that we also use to help us construct our own. By examining these therapeutic metaphors, we can learn something about our representations of ourselves as therapists in relationship with our patients and evaluate whether and in what ways these metaphors serve or hinder our patient's interests.

Freud (1912b) offered the therapeutic metaphor of the surgeon-patient relationship to his disciples and fellow psychoanalysts. Freud (1915) elaborated on this metaphor in his paper on transference-love, in which he seemed to be defending against the intensity of his female patients' professions of love with a sterile, rigid set of technical guidelines. Humanistic psychologist Carl Rogers (1977) offered a radically different therapeutic metaphor of the person-person relationship, the egalitarianism of which stands in stark contrast to Freud's authoritarianism (see also Vitz, 1977). We might consider Rogers's therapeutic metaphor a reaction to the rigidity of classical psychoanalytic technique in vogue at the time. With the advent of attachment theory (e.g., Bowlby, 1973, 1980, 1982, 1988) and the psychoanalytic study of mother-infant interaction (e.g., Bowlby, 1958, 1973, 1980, 1982; Mahler, Pine, and Bergman, 1975; Stern, 1977, 1985, 1995; Winnicott, 1960, 1965), a new therapeutic metaphor was born: the caregiver-infant attachment relationship.

Contemporary psychoanalysts are using this metaphor to illuminate aspects of the therapist-patient relationship obscured by the Freudian metaphor such as the therapeutic components of nonverbal interactions between therapist and patient, the corrective emotional experience (Alexander and French, 1946), and the noncomplementarity of the therapist-patient match (Bernier and Dozier, 2002).

Bowlby (1977b, 1988) applied his own ideas about human attachment to the metaphor of the mother-infant relationship. He believed that the primary purpose of the therapist is to provide the patient with a secure base from which he or she can explore himself or herself and his or her relationships with others. In attachment theory, the secure base in the person of the caregiver serves the function of providing protection for the infant as he or she explores the environment. The caregiver's safe haven, a complementary concept, serves the function of comfort when internal or external threats to homeostasis cause the infant to become distressed. Concepts similar to secure base identified by other writers include conditions of safety (Weiss and Sampson, 1986), atmosphere of safety (Schafer, 1983), and background of safety (Sandler, 1960). The therapeutic relationship proceeds when the patient uses the therapist to explore oneself and one's relationships with others and for comfort when confronted by distressing internal and external threats.

Attachment theory and research have spawned the application of still other facets of the caregiver-infant attachment relationship to the therapist-patient relationship (Amini et al., 1996; Diamond et al., 1999; Diamond, Clarkin, et al., 2003; Diamond, Stovall-McClough, et al., 2003; Farber, Lippert, and Nevas, 1995; Holmes, 1996, 1998; Lyons and Sperling, 1996; Mackie, 1981; Mallinckrodt, 2000; Mallinckrodt, Gantt, and Coble, 1995; Mallinckrodt, King, and Coble, 1998; Mallinckrodt, Porter, and Kivlighan, 2005; Mitchell, 1999). Parish and Eagle (2003) identified seven facets in addition to secure base and safe haven: proximity seeking, separation protest, stronger/wiser, availability, strong feelings, particularity, and mental representation. Proximity seeking refers to the infant's need to seek proximity to the caregiver for protection when faced with an internal or external danger (Bowlby, 1982). Parish and Eagle (2003) did not define proximity seeking for the therapist-patient relationship; however, we might regard a patient's request for additional sessions after a therapist or patient vacation as an adult form of proximity seeking. Separation protest refers to the distress experienced by the infant when separated from the caregiver and the infant's protest against it (Bowlby, 1982). In the therapist-patient relationship, the patient might protest against a therapist's upcoming vacation. One of the ingredients of an attachment relationship, according to Bowlby (1977a), is that the infant perceives the caregiver as stronger or wiser than he or she is. Similarly, in the therapist-patient relationship, the patient perceives the therapist as having knowledge of the patient's problems and ways to resolve them that exceed the patient's own knowledge. Availability refers to the caregiver's emotional and physical availability to meet the infant's attachment needs (Bowlby, 1982). The therapist also meets the patient's emotional needs through attentive listening, regularly scheduled appointments, interpretations that foster a sense of being understood, and many other manifestations of therapist availability unique to each therapist-patient dyad.

An infant also expresses strong feelings toward a caregiver (Bowlby, 1982). The infant is looking for the caregiver to facilitate the regulation of these strong feelings so that he or she can begin to tolerate them. The patient also looks to the therapist for assistance with strong feelings stimulated by the therapist-patient relationship. Freud (1915) described the patient's strong feelings of romantic love for the therapist, although he did not view them as products of an attachment relationship. Particularity refers to the preference for the primary caregiver over other persons, which begins practically from birth. Infants at ten days have shown a preference to feed from the primary caregiver over a substitute (Burns, Sander, Stechler, and Julia, 1972). Patients demonstrate the same preference for their therapists. A therapist covering for a vacationing therapist meets with the vacationing therapist's patient only in an emergency. In other words, therapists are not interchangeable. Mental representation refers to the child's reliance on an internalized image of the caregiver for comfort or guidance in the caregiver's absence (Bowlby, 1973; Mahler et al., 1975). The patient also relies on this internalized image of the therapist in certain situations outside therapy. When one of my patients diagnosed with borderline personality disorder gets an urge to drink alcohol, an image of my asking her what she is feeling at that moment comes into her mind. Mental representation resembles safe haven as an internalized image of comfort when internal or external threats arise.

Another clinical concept from the psychoanalytic literature thought to reflect facets of an attachment relationship between the therapist and patient is the "working alliance" (e.g., Greenson, 1965; Mackie, 1981). Freud (1912a) foreshadowed the concept in his discussion of the dynamics of transference. He defined three components of transference: a negative component, a positive component, and an "unobjectionable" component (p. 105). The first two components are unconscious, and serve as resistances to the treatment, while the third component consists of friendly or affectionate feelings admissible to consciousness, which serves the treatment as its "vehicle of success" (p. 105). The unobjectionable positive transference represents "a belief in the value of treatment, based on widely held views of analysis as a discipline and of the analyst as a professional practitioner [which] facilitates the work" (J. Greenberg, 2001a, p. 367). J. Greenberg (2001a) has questioned whether

Freud's concept has stood the test of time and has argued that the patient enters treatment seeking a relationship rather than a professional practitioner who simply relieves symptoms.

Regardless of whether the patient is seeking a practitioner or a relationship, the concept seems to encompass a sense of trust in the benevolence of the therapist who "exhibits a serious interest" in and "sympathetic understanding" for the patient over time and establishes a "proper rapport" with him or her (Freud, 1913, pp. 139, 140). Using Parish and Eagle's (2003) list of attachment concepts applicable to the therapist-patient relationship, strong feelings, stronger/wiser, secure base, and availability either are implicitly or explicitly present in Freud's original idea. Freud (1913) suggested that the patient's attachment to the therapist is a prerequisite for the emergence of the unconscious components of transference: "[The patient] will of himself form such an attachment and link the doctor up with one of the imagos of the people by whom he was accustomed to be treated with affection" (pp. 139, 140). The link between the unobjectionable positive transference and the caregiver-infant attachment relationship is implied.

Freud's (1912a) original concept reemerged in the literature as "the therapeutic alliance" (Zetzel, 1956) and "the working alliance" (Greenson, 1965). These terms were defined as capturing elements of the real relationship to the therapist not distorted by transference. Horvath and Greenberg (1989) later sought to measure this working alliance by constructing the Working Alliance Inventory (WAI), which consists of three subscales—task, goal, and bond. "Task" refers to the level of agreement between the therapist and patient about what to do in sessions. "Goal" refers to the level of agreement about the desired outcome of treatment. "Bond" refers to the level of positive personal feelings between patient and therapist. The "bond" subscale most closely resembles Freud's (1912a) original definition of the unobjectionable positive transference. Research has repeatedly identified the working alliance as highly predictive of successful treatment outcome (Bordin, 1994; Horvath and Symonds, 1991; Luborsky, 1994; Martin, Garske, and Davis, 2000; Safran and Muran, 2000). Recently, the concept of the working alliance has been associated with the concepts of secure attachment and transference because all three concepts seem to reflect similar mental representations, affects, and strategies for affect regulation (e.g., defensive processes and interaction structures) activated by the relationship with the therapist and its correspondence with relationships with past caregivers (Bradley, Heim, and Westen, 2005; Westen and Gabbard, 2002). Whether these concepts conceptually overlap or operate at different levels of abstraction is a matter of debate (see p. 38ff).

Of course, every metaphor has a breaking point—a point at which the contours do not precisely fit. Such is the case with the metaphor of the caregiver-infant attachment relationship. The therapist is not a caregiver per se, nor is the patient an infant. The therapist provides a service paid for by the patient, which takes place in a limited time. These treatment arrangements ironically both allow the metaphor to exist and immediately invalidate it. One of my patients diagnosed with borderline personality disorder revealed a fantasy—concretely experienced by her as an expectation—that therapists should not charge for their services. In fact, in her mind, therapists have taken a vow of poverty like Mother Teresa to conduct this work. By informing her that I would be raising my fee next year, I was invalidating this fantasy. She immediately reminded me that she had abruptly ended her previous treatment when she discovered that her therapist, who wanted to raise the patient's fee to $80 per session, drove a Mercedes Benz. The fantasy of the all-nurturing, selfless caregiver conflicts with the reality of the professional aspects of the relationship. We are still working on this issue of my projected fee increase and its meanings for her.

The therapeutic relationship is unique because of financial, temporal, spatial, logistic, and ethical boundaries—boundaries that do not exist in the caregiver-infant relationship (Farber, Lippert, and Nevas, 1995; Goodman, 2006). We can imagine an Orwellian world in which the mother says to the infant, "Time's up! You've had your fill of milk for the day." Or, "Stop being a baby and get off my lap!" Or, "You can't sleep in my bed; you'll get too used to that!" Anyone familiar with ferberization techniques (Ferber, 1990, 2006) will recognize the sound of these statements offered by some behaviorally oriented psychologists already applying the model of the therapeutic relationship to child-rearing practices well suited to the regimented corporate world these children are being fitted for. The establishment of boundaries such as time, money, and, perhaps most important, therapist availability between sessions structures the therapeutic relationship in interesting ways. The expectations of contact-maintenance, caressing, fondling, holding, and primary caregiver preoccupation—all provided to the infant gratis—do not apply in the therapeutic context.

These arrangements—unique to the therapeutic relationship—might differentially affect patients according to their quality of attachment. A preoccupied patient (entangled in parental relationships from childhood) might respond to these boundaries with indignation and resentment and create an interaction structure in which he or she perceives the caregiver/therapist as withholding of emotional supplies. A dismissing patient (dismissing of the importance of parental relationships from childhood), on the other hand, might feel a sense of relief that strict therapeutic boundaries are in place—at least until the defensive processes against closeness with the therapist are analyzed. The therapeutic boundaries established by the therapist—fee, schedule, unavailability outside of session, lack of physical contact—are unilateral decisions that structure the responses that patients of various attachment patterns will have toward the therapy. These parameters do not exist in the caregiver-infant relationship. As therapists, we must be aware of the differential effects of these parameters on our patients, which can provide us with diagnostic and attachment-related information and strategies for intervention. The manner in which we establish and maintain these boundaries reflects our own use of secondary attachment strategies (deactivating/dismissing vs. hyperactivating/preoccupied), which interact with our patients' strategies to create unique interaction structures that can facilitate or hinder the treatment.

In addition to the parameters inherent to every therapeutic relationship, factors such as gender and race also make important contributions to the construction of the therapeutic relationship that might interact with the patient's quality of attachment in interesting ways. Following the work of Jessica Benjamin (1987), the resolution of the Oedipus complex for little boys in Western society often results in a rigid identification with the father and a wholesale repudiation of the mother and, by extension, women, femininity, and dependency. Whereas the mother in infancy is typically perceived as the all-powerful primary caregiver—the secure base and safe haven—this mental representation of the mother changes as the infant enters the preschool years. Boys no longer perceive her as all-powerful and all-protecting—the hallmarks of felt security—but rather as a diminished presence in the household in comparison with the father. This transformation of the maternal representation could have an impact on the patient's perception of the female therapist. One might be less likely to feel secure in a therapeutic relationship with a woman whom society has deemed "less than." Farber and Geller (1994) have observed, "Our culture seemingly 'allows' women to serve as protectors of infants and young children but not to inhabit roles that require the provision of wisdom, strength, or protection of adults" (p. 206).

How might this clinical situation interact with the patient's attachment pattern to create a particular interaction structure? Perhaps having a female therapist would exacerbate the feelings of insecurity of the preoccupied patient and elicit the devaluing tendencies of the dismissing patient. Alternatively, a female therapist might provide a welcome contrast to a diminished maternal representation from childhood. These hypotheses need to be submitted to empirical testing before any definitive conclusions can be drawn regarding the interaction between the patient's quality of attachment and the therapist's gender. It is instructive to consider these issues, however, as we observe our patients forming specific attachment relationships to us.

Similarly, the therapist's race also makes an important contribution to the construction of the therapeutic relationship. Bowlby's (1977a) imperative that the infant seek an attachment figure perceived as stronger or wiser becomes complicated when applied to the therapeutic relationship because by the time the patient reaches our office, he or she has already had a series of socialization experiences in the wider world that shape their perceptions of us as therapists situated in a particular gender, race, and class. Can an African American therapist provide a secure base for a white patient who has been chronically exposed to the pervasive injustices visited on African Americans in this country? Certainly, African American therapists *can* provide a secure base and safe haven for white patients, but for some white patients, their socialization process into the dominant culture—that still contains vestiges of racism—might present challenges to perceiving a therapist from a historically oppressed culture as stronger or wiser. The reaction of a white patient to a therapist of color might also depend on that patient's attachment quality. A preoccupied patient's insecurity and a dismissing patient's devaluing tendencies might be elicited in this arrangement. Conversely, a patient from a historically oppressed culture might have difficulty trusting in a white therapist, who belongs to a culture historically identified with wielding its authority to oppress rather than to help. This dynamic can be construed in different ways, depending on the patient's attachment quality.

Financial disparities between therapists and patients also stimulate both conventional and idiosyncratic assumptions about social class, privilege, and access to valued commodities such as education, medical coverage, and an affluent living environment. These disparities can provoke feelings of admiration, competitiveness, envy, worthlessness, grandiosity, devaluation, anxiety, or guilt—in us as well as our patients. McWilliams (1999) has solved this problem for herself by charging her wealthy professional patients whatever fee they charge in their own professions. Which feelings are likely to emerge in treatment because of financial disparities depends in part on the patient's preferred attachment strategy and our own. We as therapists need to pay attention to how such nonattachment dynamics interact with preexisting attachment patterns in both our patients and ourselves to produce unique interaction structures.

One of the most important differences between the therapist-patient relationship and the caregiver-infant attachment relationship is the difference in the mental organization of the patient versus the infant. Infant internal working models consist of expectations of caregiver responses to situations that activate the infant's attachment system (loss, separation, fear, stress, injury, fatigue, illness, and punishment) as well as the infant's responses to these caregiver responses (Bowlby, 1973; Main, Kaplan, and Cassidy, 1985). Episodic memories of these caregiver responses are consolidated into semantic memory—a more generalized, abstract memory that permits expectations to form. From these expectations, the infant can begin to predict future responses and adjust his or her behavior accordingly to increase the probability of terminating the attachment system when activated and eventually returning to exploration. These initial expectations, constructed through the accumulation of early experiences of caregiver-infant interaction when the attachment system is activated, form the foundation of the internal working model (see also Stern, 1985, pp. 97–99). Eventually, these expectations become generalized across interactions with other persons over time and become organized into a personality organization with its own quality of self- and object representations, preferred defensive processes, pattern of relating with others, and affect regulation strategy (Goodman, 2002). An infant, however, lacks this sophisticated mental organization.

When a patient enters treatment with us, we are interacting with someone who has already developed a sophisticated mental organization that that patient wants to change. The infant, however, has no such historically structured mental organization. The expectations of caregiver responsiveness are just beginning to form through countless caregiver-infant experiences day after day. In other words, "the infant is developing his or her past" (Tronick et al., 1998, p. 297).

This conceptual difference between the infant's and patient's mental organizations becomes problematic when the patient applies his or her historically developed internal working model to the therapist as caregiver. According to Dozier and Bates (2004), "Expectations of the therapist may have little to do with the therapist's actual availability, thus, the therapist must be more than sensitive to the client's needs" (p. 173). The patient signals attachment needs according to the preexisting template formed during interactions with the original caregiver, not necessarily according to the way the therapist would be naturally inclined to respond to those needs. From an attachment perspective, one of the primary tasks of psychotherapy is to change these expectations so that a patient will develop new expectations—culminating in a conscious or unconscious awareness—that his or her wishes and affects will always find containment in the mind of the therapist. The therapist is not helping an infant develop expectations of containment from scratch but rather helping a patient change current expectations—already formed over years of experience with the original caregiver—to facilitate both self-containment of affect and mutual containment of affect through interdependence with significant others.

Consistent with this reasoning, Dozier and Tyrrell (1998) suggest that "the mother's task is easier than the therapist's because she need not compensate for the failures of other attachment figures.... The task of therapy is often made more difficult because of the client's previous experiences with unavailable or rejecting caregivers" (p. 222). Caregivers of infants placed in foster care most clearly illustrate this conundrum. Often abused or neglected, these infants are placed with caregivers who need to be not only sensitive to their needs but also therapeutic; in other words, "[foster] mothers need to see their infants as needy even though the behavioral evidence might suggest otherwise" (p. 244). Thus, the metaphor of the caregiver-infant attachment relationship does not precisely fit the parameters of the therapist-patient relationship because of (1) the patient's historically determined internal working model (i.e., mental organization) and (2) the therapist's therapeutic task that transcends mere emotional sensitivity and encompasses a corrective emotional experience (Alexander and French, 1946).

Another difference between the metaphor of the caregiver-infant attachment relationship and the therapist-patient relationship is the patient's acquisition and use of language. While the infant communicates through nonverbal channels such as crying, smiling, frowning, and gesturing, the patient communicates through symbolic play or language (in most forms of psychotherapy). Indeed, Freud (1910a) labeled his treatment "the talking cure" (p. 13) at the suggestion of a patient. Of course, interpretation, mediated by language, is also the vehicle he used to cure the patient. Lacan (1977) believed that the language of the father, or "the third," broke up the symbiotic relationship of mother and infant and facilitated differentiation. Symbolization creates a distance between the signifier—the word or other symbolic representation—and the signified—the thought or feeling behind the word or other symbolic representation. The communication that occurs between the caregiver and infant, however, is presymbolic. The mechanisms by which this presymbolic communication is processed in the infant's mind are not precisely known.

Members of the Process of Change Study Group in Boston have attempted to unravel this mystery. They have classified this early experience of communication as "relational procedural knowledge" and the later experience of communication as "symbolic knowledge" (e.g., Lyons-Ruth, 1999; Stern et al., 1998; Tronick et al., 1998). This group has suggested that relational procedural knowledge—the knowledge about relationships that an infant acquires in close, face-to-face interactive communication with a caregiver—develops prior to symbolic knowledge—the knowledge about relationships represented through verbal communication. Both kinds of knowledge continue to develop throughout the course of childhood. Classical psychoanalysis has targeted the domain of symbolic knowledge for therapeutic change; however, this method ignores the domain of implicit procedural knowledge formed prelinguistically. This presymbolic form of knowledge comprises the essence of attachment patterns manifested by twelve-month-old infants with expressive vocabulary words numbering in the single digits. Implicit procedural knowledge tends to reveal itself in therapist-patient interaction structures not readily available to symbolic representation—known by contemporary psychoanalysts as "enactments" (McLaughlin, 1991). According to this group, sustained therapeutic change occurs primarily within the domain of implicit relational knowledge, not verbally mediated symbolic knowledge: "Retranscription of implicit relational knowing into symbolic knowing is laborious, is not intrinsic to the affect-based relational system, is never completely accomplished, and is not how developmental change in implicit relational knowing is generally accomplished" (Lyons-Ruth, 1999, p. 579). Thus, psychotherapy, according to this point of view, needs to conform to the metaphor of the caregiver-infant attachment relationship by emphasizing change in the nonsymbolic, procedural forms of knowledge.

Working from the same assumptions, Eagle (2003) offered a pessimistic view of therapeutic change occurring within the domain of implicit procedural knowledge: "Procedural rules are especially recalcitrant. . . . [They] do not change that readily—even in successful treatment" (pp. 45, 46). Instead, Eagle and Wolitzky (2006) suggested that therapeutic change through interpretation and acquisition of insight ("second order change," p. 14) occurs more frequently than therapeutic change through implicit procedural knowledge ("first order change," p. 14). Insight into the causal processes associated with maladaptive patterns of behavior can serve to limit these behaviors, but the desire to engage in these behaviors usually remains because first-order change has not occurred.

While these theoreticians have perhaps diminished the exclusive importance of "the talking cure" in favor of the contributions that therapist-patient enactments can make to therapeutic change, other theoreticians have argued that caregiver-infant communication can serve the purposes of intrapsychic connectedness and differentiation for the infant—even before language acquisition. Benjamin (2002) described a pattern of communication that the caregiver and infant simultaneously create and surrender to, which Aron (2006) has since labeled "a rhythmic third" (p. 356). This third quality of the interaction between the caregiver and infant creates a sense of connectedness between the dyadic partners.

Benjamin (2004) contrasted this rhythmic sense of connectedness with a sense of differentiation originating in the caregiver's marking of the infant's affective displays. Gergely (2000; see also Fonagy et al., 2002) has suggested that the sensitive caregiver mirrors the infant's negative affective displays in such a way that the infant "knows" that the caregiver is not actually experiencing the same affect but rather is recognizing and empathizing with the infant's affect. He labeled this experience "marking." A caregiver's unmodulated mirroring of the infant's affective experience (as when the caregiver expresses fright when the infant expresses a fearful response), or not mirroring the infant's affective experience at all (as when the caregiver ignores the infant's fearful response), would equally threaten the infant's sense of security. In other words, the caregiver might exaggerate some aspect of the infant's affective display to mark it as belonging to the infant rather than the mother, but signifying that the mother understands what the infant is experiencing. Marking is the process through which the caregiver contains and metabolizes the infant's dysregulated affects (for an object relations perspective on the same phenomenon, see Bion, 1962, 1967). These repeated experiences of marking facilitate intrapsychic self-object differentiation and affect regulation for the infant before the acquisition of language occurs.

It is unclear whether marking unarticulated affective displays would have the same differentiating and affect-regulatory properties after the acquisition of language. Aron (2006) suggested that the therapist's verbally mediated reflections on the patient's thoughts and feelings—presented in modulated form that resembles marking—allow the patient to identify with an image of the therapist thinking about her. Fonagy et al. (2002) might modify this conceptualization by suggesting that the patient identifies instead with a more modulated image of herself contained in the therapist's mind, which the patient then internalizes as an integrated self-representation. Both these conceptualizations apply the idea of marking, borrowed from the caregiver-infant relationship, to linguistic communication between the therapist and patient. If marking occurs during the presymbolic period of relational procedural knowing, then how can language—symbolic communication—"speak" to this layer of human experience?

Lyons-Ruth (1999) tried to answer this question with evidence from the Adult Attachment Interview (AAI; George and Solomon, 1996), which purports to measure "enactive procedural representations" (Lyons-Ruth, 1999, p. 585). The interviewee reveals these representations in verbal dialogue on the AAI but does not necessarily symbolically represent them—"even though they may be symbolically represented by the observing researcher or psychoanalyst" (p. 585). Therapeutic change, then, would occur when the therapist uses language as a vehicle to produce the marking of dysregulated affects to facilitate their modulation and containment. Thus, the metaphor of the caregiver-infant attachment relationship might still be relevant to the therapist-patient relationship if we view language as a conduit for communicating both connectedness and differentiation to facilitate the patient's affect regulation and self-object differentiation.

The following clinical example illustrates this process in the therapist-patient relationship. A therapist who marks a patient's feelings of resentment toward a family member places the feelings in an intentional frame of reference without himself or herself becoming resentful. The modulated manner in which the therapist talks about the resentment—understands the intentions of all parties involved—suggests to the patient that the therapist both understands the resentment (which facilitates connectedness between patient and therapist) while not himself or herself reacting with resentment (which facilitates differentiation between the patient and therapist). The patient begins to identify with either an image of the therapist thinking about him or her (Aron) or an image of himself or herself contained in the therapist's mind (Fonagy and his colleagues). The patient then internalizes either image or both images to facilitate affect regulation. The therapist's use of language to communicate with and change the implicit procedural level of knowledge requires both symbolic and nonsymbolic mental processing. Although "procedural systems influence and are influenced by symbolic systems through multiple cross-system connections" (Lyons-Ruth, 1999, p. 580), these neurocognitive and affective pathways are not clearly understood by psychoanalysts or attachment researchers. Functional magnetic resonance imaging (fMRI), positron emission tomography (PET scan), and other neuroimaging techniques are beginning to reveal these interconnections using clever, sophisticated research methodologies (Schore, 2003).

The final important difference between the metaphor of the caregiver-infant attachment relationship and the therapist-patient relationship concerns the difference between the infant's feelings toward the caregiver and the patient's feelings toward the therapist. We label the infant's feelings "attachment" and the patient's feelings "transference." Are these phenomena conceptually identical, overlapping, or separate? If they are separate, do they mutually influence each other or operate as parallel systems? While a conceptual relation between the infant's attachment to the caregiver and the patient's working alliance with the therapist has received a general endorsement in the literature (see above), a conceptual relation between attachment and transference seems more equivocal.

Whether young children develop transference in psychotherapy stimulated theoretical battles between the Kleinians and Anna Freudians in London in the middle of the last century. Melanie Klein (1927) routinely observed transference in her analysis of young children, while Anna Freud (1946) argued that transference in children does not occur because their "attachment" to their parents precludes any transfer of libido onto anyone else. This dispute has been settled in favor of transference; contemporary child psychoanalysts generally recognize transference phenomena in child psychotherapy (e.g., Altman, Briggs, Frankel, Gensler, and Pantone, 2002). If even young children can experience transference in psychotherapy, then can young children also become attached to their therapists? Or does the emergence of transference indicate that an attachment relationship has formed?

According to attachment theory (Howes, 1999), infants form attachments to one or a few persons significantly involved in their care, particularly in the attachment-activating situations mentioned above. These attachment relationships become hierarchically organized according to preference. For example, a female toddler might generally prefer sitting on her father's lap when her mother and father are present, but she might prefer the mother's lap instead after a bad spill or a frightening noise. The infant, however, might prefer the father to the grandmother or some other ancillary caregiver during similar attachment-activating moments. Clearly, we would include the mother and father on any short list of attachment figures, who have provided care for the infant during the organization of the attachment system, which lasts until eighteen to twenty-four months of age (Ainsworth, Bell, and Stayton, 1974). Can subsequent attachments form? Dozier and her colleagues (Dozier, Stovall, Albus, and Bates, 2001) found that infants placed in foster care even after eighteen months reorganized their attachment behavior around the emotional availability of their new caregivers. It is not known, however, whether these infants reorganize their attachment behaviors yet again when they are placed back with their biological mothers. Do remnants of these older mental organizations continue to linger and influence later behaviors?

In psychotherapy, the child patient is entering into a relationship with a potential attachment figure while maintaining an attachment to the parents. Unlike foster care, in which biological mothers perform little or no caregiving and foster mothers are solely responsible for the caregiving, the parents of the child patient continue their secure-base provision. In other words, the child establishes an attachment relationship with the therapist while maintaining an attachment relationship with the parents. Where does the child therapist place on the hierarchy of attachment figures who have been present in the child's life since the moment of birth?

I have used child psychotherapy to illustrate this problem of attachment to the therapist because the child does become attached to the therapist in spite of primary attachments to the parents. Just this morning, the mother of a nine-year-old male patient with oppositional defiant disorder in once-weekly psychotherapy called to tell me that a car had run over his dog. The first thing he said to his mother after learning about the unfortunate news was that he wanted to speak to me. I characterize this reaction as an attachment behavior to seek vocal proximity with me. In the same manner, adult patients become attached to therapists even though they might be involved in emotionally significant relationships. If we acknowledge that attachment is a regular part of the psychotherapy relationship, then how do we understand transference and its role in psychotherapy?

Few authors have contributed to our understanding of these phenomena. One group (Henry and Strupp, 1994; Mackie, 1981; Mallinckrodt et al., 2005) has argued that attachment and the working alliance are conceptually identical concepts in the sense that the spirit of "proper rapport" (Freud, 1913, p. 139) attaches the patient to the therapist and allows them to engage in a common task with a common goal (Horvath and Greenberg, 1989). In addition, some authors among this group have suggested that the attachment or working alliance represents aspects of the "real," ego-based relationship with the therapist, while the transference represents aspects of the distorted, unconscious fantasies of early caregivers transferred onto the therapist. The problem with this position, as I see it, is that an insecure attachment to the therapist can include distorted, unconscious processes such as forgetting payment, coming late to session, or dismissing one's feelings toward the therapist. In addition, fantasies of crawling inside the therapist's womb or blasting off into outer space (a common fantasy of an anxious-avoidant child patient of mine) seem to contain an obvious residue of attachment and the defensive processes against it.

A second group (Eagle, 2003; Lyons-Ruth, 1999; Slade, 1999) has hypothesized a conceptual equivalence between attachment and transference because implicit procedural knowledge, the essence of internal working models, is attributed to the therapist-patient relationship and the person of the therapist. For example, Eagle (2003) has regarded "transference patterns . . . as most representative of early procedural knowledge and rules" (p. 46), which Lyons-Ruth (1999, p. 585) has characterized as internal working models of attachment. Slade (1999) has modified the definition of transference so that it refers to the patient's "primary mode of relatedness" (p. 588) rather than the classical idea of a transfer of wishes and fears onto the therapist. The pattern of relating to an attachment figure, rather than the unacceptable aspects of the patient's own personality, is transferred onto the therapist and enacted in the therapist-patient relationship.

A third group (Bordin, 1994; Bradley et al., 2005; Diamond, Clarkin, et al., 2003; Parish and Eagle, 2003; Szajnberg and Crittenden, 1997) has taken the position that attachment shares elements of both the working alliance and transference and that, indeed, these phenomena mutually influence each other. Most of these authors have suggested that a positive working alliance is conceptually equivalent to a secure attachment, while a negative working alliance is conceptually equivalent to an insecure attachment. A positive transference usually occurs in the context of a secure attachment, while a negative transference usually occurs in the context of an insecure attachment. Yet a secure attachment can protect the treatment from the destructive effects of the negative transference. Diamond, Clarkin, et al. (2003) distinguished secure-base behavior in the therapist-patient relationship (the working alliance) from "recapitulated states of mind with respect to early attachment figures in the relationship with the therapist" (the transference; p. 170). Bradley et al. (2005) considered all three concepts virtually interchangeable.

I will present my own theoretical formulation of the relations among these three concepts. The working alliance includes nonattachment components, such as therapist-patient agreement on the tasks and goals of treatment, as well as a potential attachment component, the collaborative bond or rapport between the therapist and patient. This rapport, however, is not necessarily related to attachment in which the therapist is considered a secure base or safe haven. During the administration of the AAI, the interviewee's level of collaboration with the interviewer contributes to the attachment classification (Main and Goldwyn, 1994). Yet no one would suggest that the interviewee has formed an attachment to the interviewer, who is usually a stranger. The level of collaboration between the interviewee and interviewer depends on the interviewee's state of mind with respect to his or her attachment history with the childhood caregivers and on the interviewer's own level of collaboration, based on his or her attachment history.

In psychotherapy, a patient can collaborate with the therapist on their common tasks and goals without developing an attachment to him or her in the sense of relying on the therapist as a secure base or safe haven. It takes a history of therapist caregiving, delivered over months of exposure, to form an attachment to the therapist. In my view, treatment approaches such as cognitive-behavioral therapy (CBT) offer skills training, not caregiving per se. A working alliance is formed, yet only in rare instances would a patient treated in one of these approaches form an attachment to the therapist. Thus, a working alliance is a necessary but not sufficient condition for an attachment to form—regardless of whether the attachment is secure or insecure. The quality of the working alliance depends on the patient's state of mind with respect to attachment to the historical caregivers and on the therapist's own state of mind with respect to his or her own attachment history (Tyrrell et al., 1999), not on the patient's state of mind with respect to attachment to the therapist (see figure 3.1). As discussed on p. 49ff, noncomplementary states of mind between the therapist and patient produce a greater working alliance than complementary states of mind. The reasons for this finding are not clearly understood, but one theory is that a therapist with a noncomplementary state of mind is better equipped to facilitate the patient's affect regulation than a therapist with a complementary state of mind.

"Transference" refers to the process of transferring onto a contemporary person feelings that originally applied, and still unconsciously apply, to a person from childhood in whom the person had made an emotional investment (Freud, 1912a). The person from childhood, however, does not have to be a caregiver. Freud (1912a) stated that the "father-imago," or father object representation, represents one childhood prototype on which transference is based, "but the transference is not tied to this particular prototype: it may

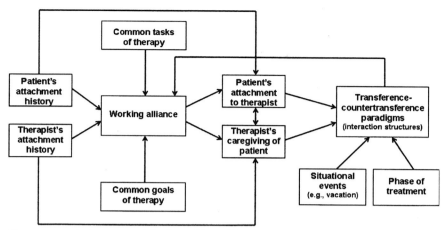

Figure 3.1. Pathways Model of Working Alliance, Patient's Attachment to Therapist, Therapist's Caregiving of Patient, and Transference-Countertransference Paradigms

also come about on the lines of the mother-imago or brother-imago" (p. 100). We know from attachment theory that an attachment is formed to a person who gives care in situations in which the attachment system is activated (see earlier discussion). Unless a sibling is sufficiently older to provide such care, we would not expect a sibling to use another sibling as a secure base. Thus, siblings do not form attachments to each other in this restricted sense of the word "attachment." Consequently, the phenomenon of transference cannot be conceptually equivalent to the phenomenon of attachment.

Indeed, there is positive and negative transference and maternal and paternal transference (Freud, 1912a) and, more recently, organizationally based transference: psychopathic, paranoid, and depressive transference (Kernberg, 1992), and idealizing and mirroring transference (Kohut, 1971). Furthermore, patients can exhibit different transferences at different times of the treatment or even in a single session. Kernberg and his colleagues (Kernberg et al., 1989) have discussed the rapidly oscillating transferences of patients with borderline personality disorder: at one moment, the patient might be casting the therapist in the role of a persecutor; the next moment, a longed-for caregiver; and the moment after that, a defiant child. Kernberg and his colleagues have articulated these oscillations using the language of projection of and identification with affectively linked pairs of self- and object representations from childhood. Each role portrayed by the therapist also arouses distinct countertransference reactions because the therapist has temporarily identified with the projected self or object representation. Bowlby (1980) and others (Grossmann, Grossmann, and Waters, 2005; Hamilton, 2000;

van IJzendoorn, 1995; Waters, Merrick, Treboux, Crowell, and Albersheim, 2000) have characterized the attachment construct as generally stable over time and resistant to change. Thus, if transference can fluctuate (sometimes rapidly in a single session) and can consist of feelings originally experienced with noncaregivers, then one must conclude that transference and attachment are conceptually independent entities. Indeed, therapists' ratings of their patients' negative transference were associated with patients' ratings of their secure attachment to the therapist (Woodhouse, Schlosser, Crook, Ligiero, and Gelso, 2003).

I want to argue that the attachment to the therapist, developed in the context of a working alliance (see above), in turn provides a context for the entire range of transference experiences in the therapist-patient relationship (see figure 3.1). Previously (Goodman, 2002), I argued that the preoccupied/hyperactivating and dismissing/deactivating internal working models represent two distinctly different personality organizations organized at a borderline level. According to Kernberg (1986a, 1986b), both borderline personality disorder and most narcissistic personality disorders (especially antisocial personality disorder) are organized at a borderline level. Borderline personality organization falls midway between the neurotic and psychotic levels of personality organization (Kernberg, 1996). What distinguishes the narcissistic personality disorders from borderline personality disorder is the presence of the pathological grandiose self. The pathological grandiose self is an admixture of idealized object representations and real and idealized self-representations that compensates for a lack of integration of a normal self-concept observed in borderline personality organization, which accounts for the paradox of relatively good ego functioning and surface adaptation in the presence of primitive defensive processes, such as splitting, and contaminated, barren object relationships. I drew comparisons between borderline psychopathology and the preoccupied/hyperactivating internal working model, and between narcissistic psychopathology and the dismissing/deactivating internal working model, and provided modest empirical evidence for these assertions (for recent evidence, see Westen, Nakash, Thomas, and Bradley, 2006).

Briefly, borderline psychopathology shares with the preoccupied/hyperactivating internal working model the features of extreme affect dysregulation, caregiver enmeshment, hostile dependence on significant others, and fear of abandonment. Conversely, narcissistic psychopathology shares with the dismissing/deactivating internal working model the features of affect dysregulation, dismissal or devaluation of the emotional importance of object relationships, counterdependence on others, and denial of vulnerability. These two personality organizations lack integration and complexity at the representational level and share some of the same primitive defensive processes such as splitting (Goodman, 2002, p. 66). I also argued that self- and object representations are the building blocks of these personality organizations; their level of integration and complexity reflects the overall level of the personality organization.

Transference-countertransference paradigms are affectively linked pairs of self- and object representations, with one representation identified with the patient and the other projected onto the therapist (Kernberg et al., 1989). These paradigms exist within a particular personality organization. For example, a psychopathic transference (Kernberg, 1992) is associated with the pathological grandiose self in a borderline personality organization. This transference consists of projecting the self-representation onto the therapist, whom the patient perceives as dishonest, exploitative, and ruthless. I am suggesting that this transference-countertransference paradigm could exist only within a dismissing/deactivating internal working model. Other constellations of self- and object representations belong to the domain of a preoccupied/hyperactivating internal working model. For example, the patient's projection onto the therapist of an infantile, dependent self-representation compels the patient to behave toward the therapist in a controlling-caregiving manner.

I am proposing that the personality organization constrains the range of representational pairs and, thus, the transference-countertransference paradigms that could emerge in a treatment. The personality organization/internal working model is therefore a necessary but not sufficient condition for a transference-countertransference paradigm to form (figure 3.1). In other words, the personality organization determines the level of quality, complexity, and integration of the affectively linked pairs of self- and object representations manifested in the therapist-patient relationship; however, other variables such as the therapist's personality organization/internal working model, quality of caregiving (see following paragraph), phase of treatment, and situational events (e.g., the therapist's vacation) also determine which representational pairs become activated.

I want to add here that the patient's attachment system both activates and is activated by the therapist's caregiving system, reciprocal to and parallel with the attachment system. The caregiving system, according to George and Solomon (1999), is activated when the caregiver perceives "internal or external cues or stimuli . . . as frightening, dangerous, or stressful for the child" associated with situations such as "separation, child endangerment, and the child's verbal and nonverbal signals of discomfort and distress" (p. 652). In the therapist-patient relationship, this caregiving takes the form of attentive listening; verbalization of affects, needs, and the processes that inhibit the reception of caregiving; empathy; limit-setting; affective containment; and mentalization, to name a few. These and other caregiving behaviors facilitate the patient's use of the therapist as a secure base and safe haven. George and Solomon (1999) discovered four patterns of caregiving analogous to the four patterns of attachment. It is believed that caregivers' own attachment histories determine the quality of caregiving for their children. I am arguing that the therapist's caregiving of the patient mediates the influence of the therapist's own attachment history on the patient's attachment to him or her. In addition, the patient's attachment and therapist's caregiving systems mutually influence each other (figure 3.1).

Thus, I am proposing a framework for understanding these relational phenomena (figure 3.1). The patient's and therapist's attachment histories with childhood caregivers, as well as their common tasks and goals, determine the quality of the working alliance, which, along with their attachment histories, determines the formation of an attachment with the therapist and caregiving of the patient, which, along with other variables such as phase of treatment and situational events, determines the range of transference-countertransference paradigms activated in the therapist-patient relationship. These transference-countertransference paradigms can in turn influence the quality of the working alliance (Bordin, 1994), which in turn influences the attachment to the therapist and caregiving of the patient. A negative transference, for example, might disrupt an already-tenuous collaboration between the therapist and patient, contaminate the patient's perception of the therapist as a secure base and safe haven and the therapist's self-perception as these functions, and result in termination of the treatment. This event is most likely to occur among those patients who rely on extremely unmodulated dismissing/deactivating or preoccupied/hyperactivating attachment strategies that dramatically increase the likelihood of affect dysregulation and resultant impulsive behavior when potentially dysregulating circumstances occur such as a narcissistic injury or a perceived threat of abandonment.

Psychoanalysis has traditionally targeted the transference-countertransference paradigms as the intervention point of entry by translating the patient's enactments, symptoms, associations, fantasies, dreams, and other clinical material related to the therapist into symbolic knowledge through their verbal interpretation. As indicated earlier, however, some psychoanalytic and attachment theoreticians are beginning to question the exclusivity and even the primacy of symbolic knowledge as a vehicle of therapeutic change: "Representational change may be set in motion . . . without necessarily assigning privileged status to a particular dimension, such as interpretation" (Lyons-Ruth, 1999, p. 601). According to Lyons-Ruth (1999), "development does not proceed only or primarily by moving from procedural coding to symbolic coding. . . . Making the unconscious conscious does not adequately describe developmental or psychoanalytic change" (pp. 579, 590). Thus, we might question whether targeting transference-countertransference paradigms is the only method or even the most efficient method for producing therapeutic change. I am suggesting that implicit procedural knowledge embodied in the patient's internal working model—"often neither conscious and verbalizable nor repressed in a dynamic sense" (Lyons-Ruth, 1999, p. 589)—can also change through the therapist's reliable provision of a secure base—a nonsymbolic procedural response aimed at this level of relational knowing. Although the verbal translation of unconscious, split-off self- and object representations can facilitate the integration of the patient's internal working model/personality organization and restore affect regulation, other, nonsymbolic interventions can also target the internal working model for therapeutic change.

In summary, I have argued that the metaphor of the caregiver-infant attachment relationship captures only certain features of the therapist-patient relationship—most important, the caregiver functions of secure base and safe haven. The metaphor appears to break down when the financial, temporal, spatial, logistic, and ethical boundaries of treatment are considered. I also noted the vast differences between the infant's and patient's fund of implicit procedural knowledge and linguistic knowledge. Finally, I discussed the difference between the infant's attachment to the caregiver and the patient's working alliance and transference to the therapist. I proposed that the working alliance and transference-countertransference paradigms are both conceptually independent of attachment phenomena embodied in internal working models but reflect the level of personality organization (psychotic, borderline, or neurotic) and the characteristic secondary attachment strategies (dismissing/deactivating or preoccupied/hyperactivating) used by the patient as an adult but originally developed out of caregiving experiences from childhood.

Chapter Four

The Therapist's Secure Base Provision and the Patient's Underlying Attachment Needs

No one pours new wine into old wineskins. If he does, the wine will burst the skins, and both the wine and the wineskins will be ruined. No, he pours new wine into new wineskins.

Mark 2:22

The therapist's fifth task is to enable his patient to recognize that his images (models) of himself and of others, derived either from past painful experiences or from misleading messages emanating from a parent, but all too often in the literature mislabeled as "fantasies," may or may not be appropriate to his present and future; or indeed, may never have been justified. Once he has grasped the nature of his governing images (models) and has traced their origins, he may begin to understand what has led him to see the world and himself as he does and so to feel, to think, and to act in the ways he does. He is then in a position to reflect on the accuracy and adequacy of those images (models), and on the ideas and actions to which they lead, in the light of his current experiences of emotionally significant people, including the therapist. . . . By these means the therapist hopes to enable his patient to cease being a slave to old and unconscious stereotypes and to feel, to think, and to act in new ways.

J. Bowlby, *A Secure Base: Parent-Child Attachment and Healthy Human Development*

In chapter 3, I suggested with others (e.g., Bowlby, 1988; Parish and Eagle, 2003) that one of the therapist's most important functions in producing therapeutic change is to provide a secure base for the patient. Secure base provision is not identical, however, to emotional sensitivity and responsiveness. In examining the mediating role of caregiver sensitivity in the well-established relation between the caregiver's attachment organization and the infant's attachment organization, De Wolff and van IJzendoorn (1997) conducted a meta-analytic study in which they concluded, "[Caregiver] sensitivity has lost its privileged position as the only important causal factor" (p. 583) in determining attachment security in infancy. Referred to as a "transmission gap," the modest correlation found between parenting behavior and the quality of infant attachment has puzzled attachment researchers because attachment theory asserts that caregiver sensitivity to the infant's emotional needs helps the infant develop expectations of caregiver reliability and security, which in turn coalesces into a secure attachment by twelve months.

One solution to this transmission gap is to consider only caregiving behavior in attachment-activating situations as influencing the quality of infant attachment (Cassidy et al., 2005). Secure base provision—the extent to which the caregiver provides a secure base in moments of fear, injury, or loss—determines the quality of infant attachment, not emotional sensitivity and responsiveness when the attachment system is not activated.

In the same manner, the therapist's provision of a secure base must meet the specific needs of the patient in moments of crisis. The therapist must discern these specific needs even though the patient might miscue the therapist and obscure these needs (Cooper, Hoffman, Powell, and Marvin, 2005; Eagle, 2006; K. T. Hoffman, Marvin, Cooper, and Powell, 2006). A therapist could respond to a patient in line with that patient's expectations developed from childhood experiences when the attachment system was activated, or respond in defiance of these expectations. The quality of the secure base provided by the therapist is likely to determine whether a context for therapeutic change is established.

The therapist's ability to discern a patient's attachment needs whispering beneath the din of defensive processes clamoring to distract him or her from hearing them depends on various factors—some of which have nothing to do with the patient, others of which interact with the patient's characteristics to produce interaction structures (Jones, 2000) unique to the therapeutic dyad. These interaction structures can facilitate or disrupt the therapist's secure base provision. Sometimes a therapist's own personality structures can interact with his or her clinical orientation to limit the treatment's effectiveness (Crastnopol, 2001; Kantrowitz, 1995). Whether the therapist and patient's characteristics are complementary or noncomplementary, and how this matching influences treatment process and outcome, have recently garnered considerable attention in the psychotherapy research literature. Freud's one-size-fits-all technical recommendations failed to account for therapist-patient matching that undoubtedly affects treatment outcomes.

Since Luborsky, Singer, and Luborsky (1975) first claimed that all psychotherapy models produce generally equivalent outcomes, psychotherapy researchers have attempted to identify therapist and patient characteristics that might improve treatment effectiveness. Out of over two hundred therapist and patient characteristics studied, therapist-patient matching accounts for a higher proportion of variance in treatment outcomes than any therapist or patient characteristic (Beutler, 1991). Matching on demographic variables such as gender, ethnicity, and first language is associated with successful treatment outcomes (Berzins, 1977; Beutler, Clarkin, Crago, and Bergan, 1991; Flaskerud, 1990; Nelson and Neufeldt, 1996). Similarly, matching on personal values, beliefs, attitudes, coping styles, expectations, and self-concept is also associated with successful treatment outcomes (Beutler, Crago, and Arizmendi, 1986; Nelson and Neufeldt, 1996; Reis and Brown, 1999; Talley, Strupp, and Morey, 1990).

On interpersonal variables, however, it is therapist-patient *mismatching* that produces successful treatment outcomes (Arizmendi, Beutler, Shanfield, Crago, and Hagaman, 1985; Beutler et al., 1991; Charone, 1981). For example, dissimilarity on values related to interpersonal security and sexual relationships produces successful treatment outcomes (Beutler, Pollack, and Jobe, 1978). Similarly, treatments are more effective when therapists who value autonomy are matched with dependent patients, or when therapists who value connection are matched with patients who value autonomy, than when both parties have similar interpersonal traits (Berzins, 1977). These contrasting interpersonal traits between the therapist and patient provide the patient with the corrective emotional experience (Alexander and French, 1946) required for a successful treatment outcome (Bernier and Dozier, 2002).

The therapeutic principle of noncomplementarity has also emerged in the attachment literature (Bernier and Dozier, 2002; Bernier et al., 2005; Dozier, 2003; Dozier and Bates, 2004; Dozier et al., 1994; Dozier and Tyrrell, 1998; Tyrrell et al., 1999). Dozier and her colleagues have demonstrated that noncomplementary secondary attachment strategies between case managers and patients produced more successful treatment outcomes than complementary secondary attachment strategies. In their first study (Dozier et al., 1994), twenty-seven patients diagnosed with thought or mood disorders and eighteen case managers of these patients were administered the AAI to determine their attachment patterns using the Attachment Q-Set (AQS; Kobak et al., 1993). The AQS yields data on two orthogonal dimensions: security-insecurity (primary attachment strategy) and deactivating-hyperactivating (secondary attachment strategy). Case managers were interviewed regarding their most recent interventions with their patients. These interviews were coded for depth of intervention and attention to dependency needs.

The results indicated that case managers rated as insecurely attached intervened in greater depth with the hyperactivating (preoccupied) patients than case managers rated as securely attached, who tended to intervene in less depth with these same patients. Similarly, case managers rated as insecurely attached attended to greater dependency needs of their hyperactivating (preoccupied) patients than case managers rated as securely attached, who attended to fewer dependency needs in these same patients. In their discussion, the authors concluded that securely attached case managers "seem able to attend and respond to clients' underlying needs, whereas case managers who are more insecure respond to the most obvious presentation of needs" (Dozier et al., 1994, p. 798). These insecurely attached case managers have difficulty resisting "the strong pull from the client to respond in ways that confirm existing [internal working] models" (p. 793). In other words, offering a noncomplementary relational experience to the patient is more likely to occur with a securely attached therapist because of "their willingness to intervene in ways that may be uncomfortable for themselves" (p. 798). The authors also pointed out that securely attached case managers responded more to the dependency needs of deactivating (dismissing) patients than those of hyperactivating (dismissing) patients.

This idea is consistent with Diamond, Clarkin, et al. (2003), who, in their work with patients with borderline personality disorder, "remain attuned to the often fleeting emergence of . . . secure states [of mind] that may emerge" (p. 167). Like a whisper, the need to rely on the therapist as a secure base is often hard to hear above the din of noise—the denials of dependency—that distracts the therapist from making a noncomplementary intervention. One of my analytic patients with borderline personality disorder denies that she misses me after vacations (for a full discussion of this case, see Goodman, in press-b, chapter 3). According to her, she enjoys sleeping in and not having to analyze everything. In spite of this patient's dismissing attitude, she comes four times per week, seldom misses a session, and is seldom late. She called me once to tell me that she was feeling ill and was canceling the following day's session. At our next session, she chastised me for not calling her back to check on her. It took several days for us to work through what she perceived as my unavailability to her. It is not my practice to call patients back under such circumstances, but perhaps, in retrospect, I should have called back this patient, because unbeknownst to me, she was using me as a safe haven during her illness. In subsequent sessions, she ignored such interpretations and focused instead on my "obligation" to patients to return their telephone calls. All of us have had similar experiences in our practices. The question is whether we allow ourselves to respond differentially to patients based on their secondary attachment strategies—to nurture the whisper of secure attachment behavior and its associated state of mind rather than silence it.

The therapeutic principle of noncomplementarity makes intuitive clinical sense. The therapist responds to the patient's underlying needs, not to his or her miscues (Cooper et al., 2005; Eagle, 2006; K. T. Hoffman et al., 2006) governed by defensive processes. Securely attached therapists are more likely to tolerate discomfort in the interaction and challenge the patient's characteristic mode of relatedness to others than insecurely attached therapists. Do we know, however, whether noncomplementary interventions actually produce more successful treatment outcomes than complementary interventions?

In their second study, Dozier and her colleagues (Tyrrell et al., 1999) administered the AAI to fifty-four patients diagnosed with thought or mood disorders and twenty-one case managers of these patients to determine their attachment patterns with the AQS (Kobak et al., 1993). The study design differed from the first study, however, because the case managers assessed treatment outcomes, defined as the quality of working alliance, global life satisfaction, and global assessment of functioning (GAF). Deactivating (dismissing) case managers and their hyperactivating (preoccupied) patients tended to have a higher quality of working alliance than deactivating (dismissing) case managers and their deactivating (dismissing) patients. Conversely, hyperactivating (preoccupied) case managers and their deactivating (dismissing) patients tended to have a higher quality of working alliance than hyperactivating (preoccupied) case managers and their hyperactivating (preoccupied) patients. Patients who belonged to noncomplementary dyads also experienced greater global life satisfaction and higher GAF than patients who belonged to complementary dyads. The authors (Tyrrell et al., 1999) argued that this study provides empirical evidence for Bowlby's (1988) therapeutic goal to disconfirm the patient's usual interpersonal and emotional strategies and expectations. In noncomplementary dyads, this goal is accomplished because case managers "have different ways of approaching relationships and regulating emotions than their clients. . . . The development of these more effective strategies can then lead to enhanced quality of life and better psychological, social, and occupational functioning for clients" (Tyrrell et al., 1999, pp. 731, 732).

One of the fascinating facets of this study is that therapist-patient correspondence on attachment patterns predicted treatment outcomes without any knowledge of the nature of the interventions made by the therapists. The authors (Tyrrell et al., 1999) indicated, "The therapeutic process that mediates the relationship between client–case manager attachment dissimilarity and positive treatment outcomes needs to be investigated more thoroughly" (p. 732). I suspect that affect regulation, produced by a noncomplementary correspondence on attachment patterns, occurs through behavioral as well as verbal channels of communication. A therapist's facial expressions, body language, seating arrangements, and tone of voice all communicate a level of tolerance or intolerance of a patient's pattern of affect regulation. The timing of the therapist's verbal interventions also communicates this tolerance or intolerance, irrespective of verbal content. The findings of this study suggest that a corrective emotional experience (Alexander and French, 1946), mediated by a noncomplementary correspondence on attachment patterns, produces enhanced treatment outcomes. In other words, new implicit procedural knowledge, acquired by the patient through the nonverbal affect-regulatory interactions with the therapist, can produce therapeutic change independent of the acquisition of new symbolic knowledge that can increase insight.

These important studies conducted by Dozier and her colleagues need to be replicated with skilled therapists in traditional psychotherapy settings with less disturbed patients to improve the generalizability of the results (Diamond, Clarkin, et al., 2003; Dozier et al., 1994). Toward this end, Bernier and her colleagues (2005) conducted a similar study with ninety first-year college students and ten professors who volunteered as academic counselors. The counselor-professors worked together with the students in regularly scheduled one-to-one sessions throughout the fall semester to provide mentoring and to discuss social and emotional adjustment problems. Students were administered the AAI, while counselor-professors completed a self-report attachment questionnaire. The authors assessed outcomes as students' adaptive behaviors and perceptions in mentoring and grade point average at the end of the semester. The results paralleled those of the previous studies: hyperactivating (preoccupied) students paired with deactivating (dismissing) counselor-professors tended to have more adaptive behaviors and perceptions in mentoring and higher grades than deactivating (dismissing) students paired with deactivating (dismissing) counselor-professors. Conversely, deactivating (dismissing) students paired with hyperactivating (preoccupied) counselor-professors tended to have more adaptive behaviors and perceptions in mentoring and higher grades than hyperactivating (preoccupied) students paired with hyperactivating (preoccupied) counselor-professors. Thus, Bernier and her colleagues (2005) essentially replicated the findings of Dozier and her colleagues (Dozier et al., 1994; Tyrrell et al., 1999) with a sample of college students receiving academic mentoring. Unfortunately, a self-report attachment questionnaire was administered to the counselor-professors, which renders the study's findings suspect because of the low correlation ($r = .09$) between the AAI and self-report measures of attachment (Roisman et al., 2007).

These empirical findings suggest that the therapist must respond differently to patients, depending on their mode of affect regulation. Because a therapist typically uses only one secondary attachment strategy (hyperactivating or deactivating) while his or her patients use either strategy, both complementary and noncomplementary dyadic therapy relationships will be established in any given patient caseload. With noncomplementary patients, therefore, a therapist "must have the ego strength and flexibility necessary to respond to the client . . . even if it is uncomfortable for the clinician at the time" (Dozier and Tyrrell, 1998, p. 240). If we acknowledge that "the clinician's state of mind . . . affects the client's expectation of availability" (Dozier and Bates, 2004, p. 173), then therapists need to obtain their own personal psychotherapy experience and self-analysis to acquaint themselves with their preferred attachment strategies and modes of affect regulation—something that psychoanalytic institutes have incorporated into their training programs for almost one hundred years (Freud, 1912b; Szajnberg and Crittenden, 1997).

TREATMENT MODALITY, SECONDARY ATTACHMENT STRATEGIES, AND TREATMENT OUTCOME

I want to propose that we classify not only therapists but also treatment modalities as hyperactivating or deactivating in their technical approach. In chapter 2, I argued that Freud's technical recommendations tended toward the deactivating end of the continuum. I would also classify cognitive therapy (Beck, 1976) and behavior therapy (Skinner, 1974) as treatment modalities on the extreme end of the continuum. On the other hand, primal therapy (Janov, 1970) and accelerated experiential-dynamic psychotherapy (Fosha, 2000) fall on the extreme hyperactivating end of the continuum. Object relations and relational therapies would fall somewhere in the middle, balancing affective containment with affective expression. Further exploration would probably reveal that therapists self-select the treatment modality they practice based partly on the fit between their secondary attachment strategy and the treatment modalities that share their own patterns of affect regulation. Deactivating (dismissing) therapists would be naturally attracted to treatment modalities that emphasize rationality, cognition, and distance, while hyperactivating (preoccupied) therapists would be naturally attracted to treatment modalities that emphasize irrationality, emotional discharge, and mutual closeness.

The therapeutic success of both Kernberg's (1975) and Kohut's (1971) treatment of patients with severe personality disorders, in spite of the apparently irreconcilable differences in theory and clinical technique between the two modalities, spawned controversy in the 1970s and 1980s (Glassman,

1988; Munich, 1993). Perhaps one secret to the success of both modalities in spite of their theoretical and technical differences is the patient population that each one treated and the fit that resulted between the treatment modality and the internal working model of the targeted population. It is already recognized that patients with different diagnostic features of borderline personality disorder require different treatment approaches (Munich, 1993). Kernberg, who developed his treatment modality to target patients with borderline personality disorder, used confrontation of hostile object representations (Kernberg et al., 1989) and an inflexible treatment frame (Yeomans, Selzer, and Clarkin, 1992) to achieve therapeutic results. Kohut, who developed his treatment modality to target patients with narcissistic personality disorder, used empathy (Kohut, 1984) and a flexible treatment frame (Kohut, 1981) to achieve therapeutic results.

If we assume that patients with borderline personality disorder rely on hyperactivating strategies of affect regulation and patients with narcissistic personality disorder on deactivating strategies of affect regulation (Goodman, 2002), then perhaps Kernberg's confrontational stance provides a noncomplementary therapeutic experience for patients with borderline personality disorder, and Kohut's empathic stance a noncomplementary therapeutic experience for patients with narcissistic personality disorder. In other words, these two treatment modalities succeed perhaps because each one corrects for the specific deficit in pattern of affect regulation presented by the population for which each treatment modality was designed to target: affective containment for the patients with borderline personality disorder and affective expression for the patients with narcissistic personality disorder.

In spite of the compelling evidence in support of the therapeutic benefit of noncomplementary therapist-patient matching on attachment organization, the therapist needs to engage in complementary interpersonal interactions with the patient in the early phase of treatment (Tracey, 1987; Tracey and Ray, 1984). Kohut (1984) intuitively sensed that a shift must take place from a complementary position vis-à-vis the patient to a noncomplementary position and divided these positions into two phases of treatment—the understanding phase (dominated by empathic understanding) and the explaining phase (dominated by explanation through interpretation). A noncomplementary stance, therefore, would be therapeutic only after a working alliance and an attachment to the therapist have been firmly established (see chapter 3). Under those conditions, the therapist's secure base function would permit the patient to explore with the therapist alternative models of intrapsychic and interpersonal interaction and alternative modes of affect regulation. A noncomplementary stance prior to the establishment of a working alliance and an attachment to the therapist, however, could cause the patient's false compliance or premature termination of treatment.

Although a "gentle challenge" to the patient's preferred pattern of affect regulation is associated with positive therapeutic change (Dozier and Bates, 2004, p. 174; see also Dozier, 2003), especially in long-term intensive psychotherapy where internal working models can be worked through in depth (Dozier and Tyrrell, 1998), other research groups (McBride, Atkinson, Quilty, and Bagby, 2006) have concluded that a *complementary* pairing of treatment modality with the patient's attachment pattern yields the most successful treatment outcome for patients with depression—regardless of the phase of treatment. This research group randomly assigned fifty-six patients with major depressive disorder to one of three treatment conditions—cognitive-behavioral therapy (CBT), interpersonal therapy (IPT), or medication. Patients were informed that they would be receiving sixteen to twenty sessions of treatment in the CBT or IPT condition, and "if a patient had not achieved treatment response by 20 weeks, treatment was terminated" (p. 1044). Patients completed a self-report measure of attachment at intake and two self-report measures of depression at intake and within one week of termination. Avoidant (dismissing) attachment moderated the relation between treatment condition and depression. Specifically, avoidantly attached patients paired with CBT experienced a greater reduction in depressive symptoms than avoidantly attached patients paired with IPT. McBride and her colleagues (2006) interpreted their results: CBT "may appeal to avoidantly attached individuals who may emphasize narrowly the importance of cognition as a way to remove themselves from interpersonal concerns" (p. 1051), whereas IPT "might . . . prove too threatening for individuals who regulate affect by deactivating relationship issues" (p. 1050).

This finding appears to support my hypothesis, stated earlier, that treatment modalities can function to deactivate or hyperactivate a patient's attachment system and thus underregulate or overregulate affect. Contrary to the therapeutic principle of noncomplementarity, however, CBT—a deactivating treatment modality—matched with deactivating (avoidantly attached) patients, produced a reduction in depressive symptoms. This finding is not surprising, however, when we consider the length of treatment (sixteen to twenty sessions) and the fact that patients were informed that the treatment would not continue beyond that range. Who among us would want to form an attachment to someone we would never see again after five months? I am suggesting that sixteen to twenty sessions coincides with an early, complementary phase of treatment. A working alliance has been established, but an attachment is just beginning to form. The later, noncomplementary phase of treatment begins after the attachment to the therapist has formed. During this second phase of treatment, the therapist can challenge the patient's implicit procedural knowledge through both verbal and nonverbal interactions with the patient. These noncomplementary interactions have therapeutic value precisely because the therapist is an attachment figure who observes deficits in the patient's affect regulation and uses the secure base function to modulate the intense affects that inevitably emerge in attachment relationships.

During the early, complementary phase of treatment, before an attachment to the therapist has formed, the sheer presence of a working alliance can serve to strengthen the patient's defensive processes, which in turn can reduce symptoms. Commenting on the McBride et al. (2006) study, Eagle (2006) observed, "CBT was more effective for the avoidant patients because it helped to prop up and strengthen defenses that had been failing. Or, at least, it did not threaten these defenses" (p. 1092). In the absence of an attachment to the therapist, perhaps this is all that time-limited psychotherapies can offer—support for the defensive structure through a complementary working alliance and temporary relief from symptomatology. A follow-up assessment at one year would have told us whether the patients had maintained their symptom reduction. A study of long-term psychotherapy in which patients form an attachment to the therapist would have also told us whether a noncomplementary match between the treatment modality and the patient's attachment pattern would have outperformed a complementary match of these conditions—an outcome that I would predict based on our theoretical and empirical knowledge about noncomplementary matching.

The question whether to provide the patient with a noncomplementary match or a complementary match—in both treatment modality and therapist attachment organization—is related to an earlier question I raised: To what extent do we allow the patient to experience us as a caregiver from childhood? And to what extent do we allow the patient to experience us as a new object—a secure base and safe haven? A complementary pairing of treatment modality, therapist, and patient would allow the patient to experience the therapist as an old object, a familiar object from childhood. For example, a deactivating (dismissing) therapist who refuses to explore the patient's underlying feelings related to the therapist's upcoming vacation perfectly complements a deactivating (dismissing) patient who responds to the news of the vacation by announcing that he or she will now be able to sleep in during session times. The therapist's behavior thus repeats the caregiver's behavior from childhood when the caregiver demonstrated no concern about the possible effects of her weeks-long separations from the child. On the other hand, the patient needs to experience the therapist as a caregiver from childhood first so that the therapist can then respond differently and thereby disconfirm these ancient caregiver expectations. This idea resembles Winnicott's (1971) primary task of the therapist: to survive the attacks of the patient without collapse or retaliation, which the caregivers had done.

A noncomplementary pairing of treatment modality, therapist, and patient would allow the patient to experience the therapist as a new object, an unfamiliar object from childhood that could disconfirm ancient caregiver expectations. For example, a hyperactivating (preoccupied) therapist who explores the patient's underlying feelings related to the therapist's vacation defies the expectations of a deactivating (dismissing) patient who responds by devaluing the therapist, calling him "a man with a vagina" (true story—see Goodman, in press-b, chapter 3). As Dozier and Tyrrell (1998) pointed out, it is the therapist's responsibility to respond to the patient in a noncomplementary manner, "even if it is uncomfortable for the clinician at the time" (p. 240). On the other hand, the therapist who never allows the patient to experience him or her as a caregiver from childhood never has the opportunity to defy the patient's ancient childhood expectations, and therapeutic change never occurs.

Greenberg (1986) argued for a balance between danger and safety in the analytic situation. Translated into attachment language, the therapist must allow the patient to experience him or herself as an *insecure* base from which transference-countertransference paradigms characterized by patient splitting and projection predominate. As an insecure base in the patient's eyes, how will the therapist respond? Will the therapist confirm this status with complementary behavior, or disconfirm it with noncomplementary behavior? In the previous example, I decided to explore the feelings about my vacation even though I knew my patient was going to devalue me. I needed to be an insecure base and temporarily abandon her by taking a vacation before I could disconfirm her dismissing image of me by showing concern about her feelings about it. Consciously, she needed to protect herself from my move toward connectedness (asking her about her feelings) by creating distance from me (devaluation). Unconsciously, however, she wanted me to show concern for her feelings—something she had never experienced from her childhood caregivers. Her hostile defense against closeness belies the intensity of her wish to be cared for.

POURING NEW WINE INTO OLD WINESKINS OR NEW WINESKINS?

Relational theoreticians have made us aware of the simultaneous tasks of the therapist—(1) to permit the emergence of the transference (i.e., to permit oneself to be used as an old object) and (2) to respond differently to the patient than the old objects did (i.e., behaving as a new object). How does the therapist determine when to behave like an old object and when to behave like a new one? In other words, when does the therapist behave in a complementary manner and when does he or she behave in a noncomplementary manner? First, the therapist must clinically assess the patient's attachment pattern—whether he or she tends to use deactivating (dismissing) or hyperactivating (preoccupied) strategies to interact with significant others, including the therapist. Slade (1999) has presented a superb description of these strategies as they appear in the therapist-patient relationship—what she calls a patient's "primary mode of relatedness" (p. 588). The therapist needs to know about these secondary attachment strategies because they help define what would be considered complementary or noncomplementary behavior. The therapist who calls a patient who missed a session without calling to cancel would be demonstrating complementary behavior with a hyperactivating (preoccupied) patient and noncomplementary behavior with a deactivating (dismissing) patient.

Second, the therapist must know about his or her own secondary attachment strategy because it also helps define what would be considered complementary or noncomplementary behavior. If the deactivating (dismissing) therapist's natural tendency is to withdraw emotionally and become uncharacteristically quiet after the patient devalues him or her, then the therapist needs to "be aware of and monitor one's fundamental strategies and reactions for the patient's sake" (Szajnberg and Crittenden, 1997, p. 435). Clinical training is a necessary but not a sufficient condition to facilitate noncomplementary behavior among therapists. Experienced therapists responded to patients in a complementary manner even though they had been trained to understand and resist the patient's maladaptive relational patterns (Henry, Strupp, Butler, Schacht, and Binder, 1993). Long ago, psychoanalytic training programs required candidates to "have undergone a psycho-analytic purification and have become aware of those complexes of his own which would be apt to interfere with his grasp of what the patient tells him" (Freud, 1912b, p. 116). Perhaps other treatment modalities should consider adopting a personal therapy requirement so that the therapist is in a more enlightened position to determine whether he or she is engaging in complementary or noncomplementary behavior vis-à-vis the patient's verbal and nonverbal behavior.

Third, the therapist needs to consider the phase of treatment because the therapist's response to the nature of the relationship with the patient varies with the treatment phase. As I mentioned earlier, a treatment could be divided into complementary and noncomplementary phases. The complementary phase constitutes the early phase of treatment, when the working alliance is established and an attachment to the therapist is beginning to form. The patient needs to begin to experience the therapist as a childhood caregiver—an attachment figure. After the attachment to the therapist has formed, the therapist can then move into the noncomplementary phase, when he or she begins to challenge the patient's secondary attachment strategy by facilitating either the expression of unacceptable attachment needs (for a deactivating/dismissing patient) or their containment (for a hyperactivating/preoccupied patient). In the language of Alexander and French (1946), the therapist is providing a "corrective emotional experience" (p. 294).

Fourth, the therapist needs to consider the goals of treatment because the patient might not be seeking personality change at the level of implicit procedural knowledge. Instead, the patient might simply want immediate relief from his or her symptoms. The goal of treatment might dictate that a complementary treatment phase comprise the entire course of treatment. I argued earlier that the positive outcome from a complementary interaction between CBT and deactivating (dismissing) patients with depression (McBride et al., 2006) represented the strengthening of the patient's defensive processes and subsequent symptom reduction. For patients who seek a lasting, generalized personality change, however, "long-term intensive therapy may be required" (Dozier and Tyrrell, 1998, p. 224). This intensive psychotherapy requires the therapist to adopt a noncomplementary stance vis-à-vis the patient to achieve the patient's goal of enduring personality change.

Fifth, the therapist needs to consider the length of treatment because insurance companies often do not reimburse the therapist beyond a certain number of sessions—too few for an attachment to the therapist to form. Under these conditions, the therapist can commence only a complementary phase of treatment. The insurance companies fail to understand that a corrective emotional experience can never take place because the patient is not in treatment long enough to form an attachment to the therapist. Consequently, the patient experiences only temporary relief, and when his or her benefits renew on the policy renewal date, he or she will be seeking another round of short-term treatment from the insurance company. Insurance companies could avoid funding a revolving door if they realized that it is more cost-effective to reimburse for one long-term intensive treatment that provides a corrective emotional experience than it is to reimburse for multiple short-term superficial treatments over the course of the policyholder's lifetime.

Sixth, the therapist needs to consider the patient's potential to comply with the therapist's noncomplementary stance rather than respond authentically. The patient who feels that the therapist's secure base function could fail might conform to the therapist's noncomplementary intervention just to preserve the attachment. Eagle (2003) has suggested that the patient wants not only to please the therapist but also to create a feeling of being understood and accepted. It is critical that the therapist recognize the profound power that he or she wields as a secure base and safe haven for his or her patients. For example, a patient fearful of abandonment might agree to pay the therapist a fee increase that the patient is unable to afford to prevent the therapist from carrying out what she perceives to be an imminent abandonment if she resists. The therapist's intervention is noncomplementary because it communicates to the hyperactivating (preoccupied) patient that the therapist is a separate person, has financial needs, and is temporarily relinquishing the caregiver role to assert that the patient meet these needs. The patient could comply to avoid a feared abandonment rather than authentically recognize that the therapist is indeed a separate person with a separate set of needs that exist independently of the patient's attachment to the therapist. The treatment frame (Langs, 1976; Langs and Stone, 1980) needs to be a focal point of discussion whenever the therapist or patient suggests changes to it so that the therapist can identify patient compliance and help the patient to understand it in the context of the power dynamic intrinsic to the attachment relationship.

Finally, the therapist needs to remember this paradox: to be both an old and a new object, to behave in both a complementary and a noncomplementary manner, to accept the patient's projections, and to interpret them. The effective therapist first allows the patient to transform him or her into the "ghosts in the nursery" (Fraiberg, Adelson, and Shapiro, 1975)—the imperfect attachment figures from the past—and then mentally contains the image of the patient in relation to these attachment figures by reflecting on the experience rather than reacting reflexively (Bion, 1962, 1967; Dozier et al., 1994). This mental containment detoxifies the old childhood experiences of an insecure base and unsafe haven and repairs them so that the patient can begin to use the relationship with the therapist and other meaningful relationships as a secure base and a safe haven in moments of distress. The patient thus discovers what it means to depend on a separate person for comfort and safety. The capacity to depend on others as separate persons is considered a hallmark of integrated object relations (Kernberg, 1986b).

Perhaps Casement (2001) expresses the same ideas more eloquently: "An analytic 'good object' . . . is that which can tolerate being used to represent the worst in a patient's experience . . . [and] can bear to feel that despair, along with them, and yet find the courage to go on with the analysis" (pp. 384, 385). Too often, the therapist rushes in to rescue the patient from the old objects, thereby avoiding the punishing or despondent transferences (and withdrawing or retaliatory countertransferences), and depriving the patient of an opportunity to face the ghosts. It is in the bearing of the patient's despair and "nameless dread" (Bion, 1967, p. 116)—rather than fulfilling the patient's expectation of collapsing or retaliating—that the therapist becomes a new object and adopts a noncomplementary stance vis-à-vis the patient.

Paradoxically, the precursors of this noncomplementary stance originate in the caregiver-infant relationship. Dozier and her colleagues (Bernier and Dozier, 2002; Bernier et al., 2005; Dozier, 2003; Dozier and Bates, 2004; Dozier et al., 1994; Dozier and Tyrrell, 1998; Tyrrell et al., 1999) argued that therapeutic change occurs when the therapist gently challenges the patient's expectations of how others respond to him or her in relationships. These expectations form in the crucible of the caregiver-infant relationship over the course of many experiences of care in times of distress and discomfort. If the caregiver refuses to pick up the infant when he or she is distressed, then the infant will grow up to expect no such care from anyone else. If the caregiver picks up the infant inconsistently when he or she is distressed, then the infant will grow up to expect care only when he or she dramatizes the distress. A noncomplementary stance, therefore, would be giving care when care is needed but not expected or titrating care to correspond to the actual need. Caregivers who function as a secure base and safe haven, however, also provide noncomplementary care to their infants.

In chapter 3, I discussed the concept of "marking"—the caregiver's attempt to empathize with the infant's pain and simultaneously to convey to the infant a dissimilarity in the caregiver's own affective state (Fonagy et al., 2002; Gergely, 2000). This subtle differentiation between the disorganized feelings of the infant and the organized, yet empathic, feelings of the caregiver produces the affective containment and regulation sought by the infant. How does this process relate to the noncomplementary stance of the therapist? The caregiver is neither collapsing nor retaliating against the infant's primitive affective displays but rather is responding creatively by incorporating the infant's feelings (helplessness, fear, anger) and her own feelings (concern, calmness) into a unique affective display that neither disregards the infant's feelings nor reflects them back. The caregiver marks the infant's feelings as known to her but different from her own.

The therapist also conveys an empathic understanding of the patient's affective displays but also challenges their gravity just by tolerating them—something the caregivers from childhood were unable or unwilling to do. The patient who reminded me that she had abruptly ended her previous treatment after a fee increase is struggling with the fact that her mother is asking her for money to support a lavish lifestyle (see Goodman, in press-b, chapter 3). My patient resents her mother's requests for financial support, not only because the mother does not need it, but also because she unconsciously resents her mother for physically abusing and ignoring her as a child. Because the mother never met my patient's emotional needs, my patient feels that her mother should not now be asking my patient to meet *her* needs. Resenting my projected fee increase next year, the patient has cast me in the role of the old object—her greedy, depriving mother—and herself in the role of the deprived, neglected child.

Because of the exploitative and neglectful manner in which my patient's mother treated her as a child (and continues to treat her), my patient feels entitled to compensation from caregivers, including me. In the past, she has said that mental healthcare providers, like Mother Teresa, should take a vow of poverty and offer their services free of charge. My projected fee increase contradicts her fantasy of me—and all caregivers—as a breast with infinite supplies, and refutes her expectation that she is entitled to special dispensation from her mental health caregiver. Of course, the expectation of perfect care disguises the unbearably painful underlying expectation of no care at all. I could confirm her expectation of entitlement and drop the projected fee increase, but that would not promote any therapeutic change. Proceeding with the fee increase introduces the painful awareness of reality—that I am a separate person with limitations and needs.

Using the concept of "marking," how should I proceed with my patient? I need to use my skill and creativity to show my patient that I understand and empathize with her childhood resentment, its influences on her fantasies of entitlement to omnipotent caregiving, and her painful awareness that I am separate and not omnipotent. At the same time, I need to show my patient that my understanding of these issues comes out of a position of difference—that I neither share her wish for omnipotent caregiving nor expect myself to be able to fulfill it. In other words, I am tolerating the expression of her wish without actually fulfilling it. Just this morning, this same patient requested to move up our Thursday appointment time from 7:15 a.m. to 7 a.m. because it would facilitate her work schedule (note that one of her reasons for wanting to end the analysis is to get more sleep). I agreed to the time change. At the end of the session, she asked me to remind her of the Thursday time change in Wednesday morning's session. I reflected back that it was her suggestion to change the time. She responded that she would write down the time change. I could have agreed to remind her, but then I would have been assuming the role of the omnipotent caregiver, and she the role of the perfectly cared-for child. I chose instead to invalidate her expectation, which I believe, in this patient with borderline personality disorder, will promote therapeutic growth over time. A patient with narcissistic or paranoid personality disorder might require a different therapeutic approach based on a different set of wishes and expectations.

I have been arguing that this sense of affective containment (Bion, 1962, 1967) comes about through the moment-by-moment process of "empathic emotion-reflective interactions" (Gergely, 2000, p. 1208) that consist of marking the infant's/patient's affects as understood and tolerated by the caregiver/therapist but belonging to the infant/patient. In Bion's (1962, 1967) language, the "K-link" represents the process by which the infant engages in affective communication through projective identification (see also Ogden, 1979), activating the mother's capacity to receive and modify the communication through metabolization. The infant projects hostile, persecutory "beta elements" onto the mother to control her. The emotionally responsive mother, interpreting the projective identification as a message of distress (e.g., hunger, discomfort, the need for protection), acts as a container of these primitive affects and transforms them through the "alpha function" into modulated, coherent affects. The infant then introjects these metabolized affects, thus accumulating experiences that ultimately form an object representation "capable of self-knowledge and communication between different aspects of themselves" (Britton, 1998, p. 23). Hence, the K-link serves the purpose of transforming object representations of extremely negative affective valence into integrated, modulated representations through integration with good object representations. I am arguing that this transformation of beta elements through the alpha function takes place through the moment-by-moment marking described by Gergely and his colleagues (Gergely, 2000; see also Fonagy et al., 2002).

If, as I am arguing, this process of marking is as vitally important to the psychotherapy process as it is to the caregiving process, then how does the therapist go about marking the patient's affects? Recalling my earlier discussion about implicit procedural knowledge and symbolic knowledge (see chapter 3), therapists need to target both areas to facilitate therapeutic change (Lyons-Ruth, 1999). In the symbolic realm, the therapist uses clarification, confrontation, and interpretation (Kernberg et al., 1989) to communicate to the patient his or her empathic understanding of the patient's distress as well as the differentiation between the therapist's feelings and the patient's feelings. In the clinical vignette with my patient, I was communicating to her both my empathic understanding and my separateness by announcing a fee increase and discussing it with her using the symbolic medium of words.

This increase in symbolic knowledge—what Eagle and Wolitzky (2006) have referred to as "second order change" (p. 14)—facilitates affect containment and regulation by attaching meaning to affective experiences, which binds and therefore modulates the unsymbolized affects. I expect my clarifications, confrontations, and interpretations to modulate my patient's resentment over the projected fee increase by providing a symbolic network of verbally mediated explanations for her reaction. This symbolic network of explanations should include the following: (1) her attachment to me, (2) her expectation that attachment figures should offer their services free of charge, (3) her rage, disappointment, and resentment toward her mother for returning her love with physical abuse and neglect, (4) her transfer of these feelings toward her mother onto me when I announced the fee increase, (5) her need to preserve a sense of symbiotic unity between us, (6) her sense of envy and guilt over the fact that I have helped her in my separateness, and (7) her need to avoid mourning my loss as a breast with infinite supplies. Successfully working through the patient's resentment toward me could take the form of all these explanations and many others I have not listed and have not thought of. I am making connections among all these various meanings to help build a symbolic network that my patient can then use to modulate her distressing affects and respond more reflectively to significant others who assert their separateness. Simultaneously, my patient is internalizing a therapist-patient relationship that she can retrieve during affectively charged moments to help her to regulate distressing affects.

How does this process of marking take place in the implicit procedural realm? We recall that changes in implicit procedural knowledge—what Eagle and Wolitzky (2006) referred to as "first order change" (p. 14)—facilitate affect containment and regulation by modifying the rules by which the patient organizes relational understanding—"how to do things with others" (Lyons-Ruth, 1999, p. 585). This change comes about through creating "increasingly collaborative forms of dialogue" (p. 610). Taking this perspective, enactments (McLaughlin, 1991) would constitute one form of uncollaborative dialogue.

Here is an example of an attempted enactment from my private practice (see Goodman, in press-b, chapter 2): a narcissistic patient with borderline features in four-times-per-week psychoanalysis announced that she was giving me a $5 per week fee increase (I had been charging her $135 per week). I felt simultaneously gratified and devalued by the paltry increase. When I asked her about it, she said only that she felt grateful for the progress she was making and that I deserved it. One week later, she asked whether we could begin meeting again in my former office in midtown Manhattan. I informed her that the former office was no longer available, and I wondered why she wanted to move. She responded that she was planning to move to Staten Island, and seeing me in midtown Manhattan would be more convenient for her than seeing me on the Upper East Side.

I quickly formed a hypothesis about this request and asked her whether her raising my fee had anything to do with it. With some interpretive assistance, she acknowledged that she had raised my fee to manipulate me into doing her bidding—moving my office to midtown Manhattan to treat her. This interaction is what I would call a failed enactment. What was probably therapeutic, however, was not my catching her in her attempted manipulation but rather my identifying my countertransference feelings of devaluation, realizing that she was casting me in the role of the humiliated child, and her in the role of the manipulative mother. I responded to her role as the manipulative mother without adopting a masochistic position as the patient had done in relation to her mother throughout her childhood. I could have capitulated and moved mountains to see her in midtown Manhattan. Nor did I adopt a sadistic position by assuming the role of her mother and casting her in the role of the child. I did not threaten to end the treatment but responded to her request instead with curiosity—a desire to understand what she was communicating to me. The mother had forced the patient's submission as a child by often threatening to leave home, suitcase packed and coat on. Through the clinical work, the patient could begin to see how she was treating me and relate it to her childhood relationship with her mother.

From an attachment perspective, I could interpret this enactment on an unconscious level as meaning that the patient was seeking reassurance that I cared enough about her to move my office, which would have increased my physical proximity to her. The patient, who tended to dismiss her attachment needs, was unable to ask for reassurance directly and instead attempted to enact an answer from me. Gratifying her surface needs—moving my office—would have shown her that I was, in fact, not a secure base who wants to understand her, but an insecure base who wants to please her. Retaliating against her surface needs also would have shown her that I was an insecure base who wants to punish her. Through a collaborative dialogue (Lyons-Ruth, 1999), I empathized with her need to feel closer to me as well as my need for us to continue working in my current office. One question I posed to my patient ("How does it feel to you that I will be staying in this office?") suggests a concern for her feelings even though I decided not to fulfill her request. I am saying, "I feel your feelings, but I also feel something different from you." The dialogue between my patient and me infiltrates the implicit procedural realm not through the word content, but through the intersubjective rhythm created between my patient and me (Aron, 2006).

TRANSFORMING THE DARK MATTER

In addition to enactments, what are some other ways therapists can reach the implicit procedural realm and transform it? Implicit procedural knowledge is like dark matter in the universe—invisible yet comprising the vast majority of mass in the knowable universe. The term serves as an expression of science's ignorance: no one can see dark matter, so no one can describe it. We know it exists only because science can infer it from measuring the rotations and velocities of galaxies ("Dark Matter," 2007). Because implicit procedural knowledge is unsymbolized and not conscious (Lyons-Ruth, 1999; Stern et al., 1998), we therapists cannot "see" implicit procedural knowledge either. We feel it in our conscious and unconscious countertransference reactions, in the process of the interactions with our patients rather in than their verbal content. I will attempt to outline in the following paragraph what the dark matter of implicit procedural knowledge is for me and how therapists work with it to produce therapeutic change.

The process by which the caregiver repairs ruptures in their interactions with their infant contributes to the pattern that the infant's internal working model ultimately forms (Solomon and George, 1999; Stern et al., 1998). Applied to the therapist-patient relationship, the process by which the therapist repairs ruptures in their interactions with their patient can contribute to changes in implicit procedural expectations of how others respond when a rupture in a meaningful relationship takes place. When I announced to my patient that I would be raising my fee, a rupture in the working alliance took place. How I respond to this rupture, day by day, will determine whether my patient's implicit relational knowing will shift from a general expectation of physical abuse or neglect to a less draconian one.

The therapist's reliability—his or her consistent presence—is unconsciously registered in the patient's implicit relational knowing. Aspects of the treatment frame (Langs, 1976; Langs and Stone, 1980)—punctuality, an unchanging office space, a consistent session length, day, and time, a routine billing procedure—are all background events (Stern et al., 1998) that infiltrate the patient's implicit procedural knowledge and either confirm or disconfirm the expectations contained therein. These events are not conscious—not in the sense that they are dynamically repressed (Stern et al., 1998)—but not usually noticed. The patient does not notice that the therapist starts every session on time until that one time when he or she is late. The patient must have been registering the session starts, however, because the late session start stands out in his or her mind.

How the therapist announces and discusses vacations with the patient is also registered in the patient's implicit procedural unconscious. Preparing the patient for a separation can facilitate the preservation of the therapist's secure base function for the patient and repair the expectations of rejection, emotional inconsistency, abandonment, or unavailability that emerge in the context of the therapist's (or patient's) leaving or absence. The therapist needs to remember that the patient's needs for trustworthiness, reliability, stability, and emotional availability coincide with these expectations of insecurity. The patient needs to experience their therapist as considering their attachment needs, not confirming their expectations.

The therapist's availability during emergencies also communicates security in the implicit procedural realm. Some therapists suggest minimal contact with patients with borderline personality disorder outside of sessions, and, indeed, under certain circumstances, inform the patient in advance that the patient will be terminating the treatment if he or she contacts the therapist in a life-threatening emergency (Kernberg et al., 1989). Other therapists place no such restrictions on outside contact with these patients (Linehan, 1993). Regardless of the procedures followed for availability during emergencies, the therapist needs to consider the impact of his or her response to emergencies when the attachment system is activated and the patient is seeking proximity for the sake of protection—even from oneself. The therapist's response is bound to affect the patient's implicit procedural knowledge in profound ways. When the emergency is self-destructive behavior, the therapist needs to consider whether a response to the patient's dramatically presented attachment need would represent a repetition of the pattern of the childhood caregiver to respond to the patient only in dramatic situations. Under these circumstances, the patient is forcing the therapist to behave in a complementary manner. On the other hand, if the patient knows that the therapist's policy is to respond whenever a life-threatening emergency arises, the patient might feel less of a need to make the therapist prove himself or herself as a safe haven.

Other behaviors that register in the patient's implicit procedural realm include vocal tone and prosody, body posture and gestures, muscle tone, and facial expressions. The patient might not consciously notice these emotional indicators, but they still communicate whether the therapist is functioning as a secure base and safe haven. A patient of mine became surly toward me in the middle of a session. Later in the session, I asked her whether she had noticed that her attitude toward me had shifted. She too had noticed it, but could not figure out why. Together, we traced the shift back to a comment I had made that she reasoned she must have heard as sarcastic. My patient was not aware that she had heard my comment as sarcastic, nor was she repressing the sarcastic tone she had heard. Nevertheless, it influenced her attitude toward me.

In this situation, we were able to convert the implicit procedural knowledge into symbolic, verbally mediated knowledge through an analysis of our interactions earlier in the session. As Lyons-Ruth (1999) has pointed out, however, "Retranscription of implicit relational knowing into symbolic knowing is . . . not how developmental change in implicit relational knowing is generally accomplished" (p. 579). Making this conversion to symbolic knowing made it possible for my patient and me to discuss the role I was playing for her at that moment, which increased her understanding. Our collaboration on figuring out together when and how her attitude shifted, however, communicated my secure base function to her in the implicit procedural realm. Words were a necessary substrate on which the collaboration developed, but not sufficient to register in my patient's implicit procedural realm. "Something more" (Stern et al., 1998) than the words of interpretation was needed to communicate to my patient on this "dark matter" level of knowledge.

Perhaps the most valuable way that a therapist can communicate to the patient in the implicit procedural realm is to bear the negative transference and not be crushed by it or moved to retaliate against it (see Casement, 2001; Winnicott, 1971). The therapist's secure base function in the midst of the patient's rage "speaks" to the implicit procedural realm like no verbally mediated intervention. The use of words can facilitate this secure base function, but the therapist's unwavering presence speaks even louder than words. With patients who have historically experienced words as attacks, lies, and manipulation, perhaps only the nonsymbolic channels of communication can convince these patients of the therapist's trustworthiness, reliability, and goodwill. The therapist's constant benevolent presence with the patient, whatever the emotional circumstances, might be the only mode of therapeutic change available.

CLINICAL ILLUSTRATION: DEVON

Devon, a five-year-old boy in foster care because of parental neglect and exposure to domestic violence, was seeing me in once-weekly psychotherapy (see Goodman, 2002). In one session, Devon was portraying his older brother as aggressive, hostile, and provocative—in much the same way that he had portrayed his father in previous sessions. When I interpreted that he must hate his brother for acting this way toward him, Devon looked worried and apologized. The interpretation had obviously aroused feelings of guilt. He ended our role-play and precariously perched himself on top of a chair, looking to see if I would intervene with a prohibition. When none was immediately forthcoming, Devon asked whether I was going to stop him. I interpreted that Devon was concerned about whether I was concerned enough about him to protect him from danger. Devon then got off the chair and went to the telephone. He asked if he could call 911. I interpreted that Devon was feeling as though he needed me to rescue him. Could he trust me to help him with his feelings, especially his angry feelings? Devon asked if he could press numbers other than 911. He pretended to talk to me over the telephone.

Devon wanted to know whether I would still be a secure base/safe haven for him even though he was expressing anger, which I communicated to him I knew about. I suspect that Devon expected that any expression of his anger would result in the emotional or physical withdrawal by the attachment figure—probably a historical fact in his short but eventful life. Was I going to withdraw from him like his parents, or panic like his foster mother, or pass this test (Weiss and Sampson, 1986) by demonstrating that I could be a secure base without withdrawing or panicking? I believe that I passed this particular test. Perhaps I failed other tests. Our words and behaviors as therapists need to work in synchrony to mark the patient's affects as understood by us but not exactly shared by us. I communicated simultaneously (1) my concern about Devon's worry about whether I was going to rescue him and (2) my sense that he was not in imminent danger. I believe that this interaction and many others like it produced lasting, first-order therapeutic change in Devon's implicit procedural knowledge.

Chapter Five

Assessing the Patient's Attachment to the Therapist: Three Empirical Approaches

> You will see that in the explanation of how these patients behave during analysis I have advanced a number of interlocking hypotheses. In a research programme each requires scrutiny and testing in the light of further data. . . . There remains an important place for further observations to be made during the analysis of individual patients; though I believe that, if clinical research is to yield its full potential, it has to be pursued in a far more systematic and directed way than hitherto. . . . It would also be especially valuable if we were to have a detailed account of the conditions in which a major therapeutic change occurs.
>
> J. Bowlby, *A Secure Base: Parent-Child Attachment and Healthy Human Development*

If we accept the idea that at least some aspects of the metaphor of the caregiver-infant attachment relationship apply to the therapist-patient relationship, then empirical study might help us to understand how to measure these aspects and determine whether they actually produce therapeutic change, as Bowlby (1988) suggested. As I discussed in chapter 3, the patient's attachment to the therapist is constructed out of the patient's attachment history, the therapist's attachment history, and the working alliance, which in turn consists of the goals and tasks of treatment as well as the bond between the patient and therapist (Horvath and Greenberg, 1989). I believe that this bond represents the beginning formation of the attachment to the therapist. The therapist and patient's attachment histories both directly and indirectly influence the patient's attachment to the therapist through the working alliance (see figure 3.1).

Why does the therapist's attachment history influence the patient's attachment to the therapist? Overwhelming evidence now exists to conclude that the primary caregiver's state of mind with respect to attachment, which reflects his or her attachment history, is the most significant contributor to the infant's quality of attachment by twelve months (for a meta-analysis, see van IJzendoorn, 1995). Genetic factors and temperamental reactivity are unrelated to the four attachment patterns (for a review, see Levy, 2005). Following the metaphor of the caregiver-infant attachment relationship, the therapist's attachment history must also influence the patient's quality of attachment to the therapist. The therapist's clinical technique, personality, dependability, and response to the patient's crises and range of emotional states all reflect his or her attachment history—the innumerable experiences of having been taken care of and the defensive processes used at times when he or she felt not taken care of.

The infant develops expectations from repeated experiences of caregiver responses to situations that activate the infant's attachment system (loss, separation, fear, stress, injury, fatigue, illness, and punishment) (Bowlby, 1973; Main et al., 1985). These expectations become generalized to other relationships (Stern, 1985) and ultimately contribute to a person's "primary mode of relatedness" (Slade, 1999, p. 588). Every therapist has a primary mode of relatedness that influences his or her technique and personality, dependability and characteristic response to crisis. This primary mode of relatedness is communicated to the patient by the therapist's words and other vocal expressions, facial expressions and gestures, and behaviors. Like an infant, the patient, to varying degrees, forms expectations in therapy from repeated experiences of therapist responses to attachment-activating situations (e.g., therapist vacations). The patient then accommodates these therapist responses to optimize the gratification of attachment needs. An anxious-avoidant infant avoids contact with the caregiver after a brief separation to avoid feeling rejected by a rejecting caregiver. An anxious-resistant infant exaggerates his or her affective display after a brief separation to insure comforting by an inconsistent caregiver. I am suggesting that patients also adjust to therapists' characteristic responses to attachment needs.

This model is too simplistic for explaining the formation and quality of the patient's attachment to the therapist, however, because unlike the infant, the patient has already developed an internal working model of caregiver expectations that Bowlby (1980) believed became increasingly resistant to change with development. The situation resembles the one between foster caregivers and infants placed in foster care, who have already formed internal working models of their relationships with their primary caregivers (Dozier and Tyrrell, 1998). These infants respond to their new caregivers "with expectations that help them to cope with previously problematic experiences, but which are often inappropriate in the new context" (p. 244). The authors have suggested that foster caregivers need to be not only sensitive but also therapeutic, perceiving these infants as "needy even though the behavioral evidence might suggest otherwise" (p. 244). Similarly, patients come to therapy with expectations that helped them to cope with previously problematic experiences from childhood but that have outlived their usefulness. These "inappropriate" expectations—perfect love, torture, abandonment, rejection, unreliability, omnipotent protection, exploitation, criticism—contribute to the caregiving environment of therapy. Thus, both the therapist and patient's attachment histories contribute to the formation and quality of the therapist-patient relationship. Just as infants placed in foster care must explore "alternative working models of caregiver availability" (p. 244), so too must patients explore alternative working models of therapist availability, because the therapist is not likely to behave like the caregivers from childhood.

Before reviewing three empirical approaches to assessing the patient's attachment to the therapist, I want to address two issues: (1) the length of time it takes to form an attachment to a caregiver and (2) self-report measures of attachment. Bowlby (1980) believed that infant attachment becomes organized as a behavioral system directed toward the primary caregiver by approximately nine months. Infants placed in foster care from birth to twenty months and living there from three to twenty-one months manifested attachment patterns between twelve and twenty-four months that reflected the attachment state of mind of their foster caregivers (Dozier, Stovall-McClough, Albus, and Bates, 2001). These results suggest that these infants changed their expectations to conform to the new caregiving experiences created by the foster caregivers in as little as three months. Unfortunately, the authors did not report whether time spent in foster care increased the probability of change in attachment quality. Considering the fact that internal working models are increasingly resistant to change (Bowlby, 1980), we would expect a longer gestation period for attachment to form and change in older children and adults. Thus, we need to ask the question, after how many sessions does a patient become attached to a therapist?

A patient needs to be able to perceive the therapist as a secure base from which to explore his or her thoughts and feelings and a safe haven to which he or she can return for comfort (Bowlby, 1988). I imagine that this process takes time. No one knows how long. None of the empirical studies I will be reviewing has addressed this question. The rate at which an attachment to the therapist forms probably depends on many factors, including the attachment histories of the patient and therapist, the negotiated length and frequency of the treatment, and the extratherapeutic circumstances of the patient (e.g., death of a parent). A psychoanalytically informed treatment of high frequency (multiple times per week) and open-ended termination date that commences in the aftermath of the death of a parent will be more intense than a cognitive-behaviorally informed treatment of low frequency (once per week) and a fixed termination date (ten sessions) that commences to help the patient quit smoking. I am suggesting that this therapeutic intensity would increase the rate at which an attachment to the therapist will form. In other words, I would expect these two constructs—therapeutic intensity and rate of attachment formation—to be positively correlated with each other.

One of the arguments one can make against managed care limits on the number of covered outpatient sessions and against time-limited therapies in general (which include most manualized treatments) is that an insufficient time has passed for the patient to form an attachment to the therapist. If we assume that implicit procedural knowledge changes only in the context of an attachment relationship, then none of these therapies presents an opportunity for this kind of deep personality change. If the patient wants only immediate relief from his or her symptoms, then these time-limited therapies might be helpful. On the other hand, if the patient wants a meaningful experience that could bring lasting peace of mind and changes in the primary mode of relatedness, then a longer, more intense treatment where an attachment has a chance to form would be indicated.

My position is at odds, therefore, with Mallinckrodt and his colleagues (Mallinckrodt et al., 2005), who reasoned, "At least four sessions are required to form a reasonably secure attachment" (p. 87). I am suggesting that the formation of an attachment, where the person seeks protection from potential internal or external danger by seeking emotional proximity and contact to someone considered stronger and wiser, takes longer than three hours (four sessions × forty-five minutes per session). The treatment intensity, as defined earlier, would directly affect the time needed for the patient to form an attachment to the therapist. If infants require a minimum of three months of almost constant caregiver contact, then we would expect attachment formation in adults to take longer than three hours.

Each of the three research groups who have studied the patient's attachment to the therapist has defined the length of treatment differently for measuring this construct. Mallinckrodt and his colleagues (Mallinckrodt et al., 2005, p. 89) studied patients who had completed between four and eight sessions of a twelve-session treatment, whereas Parish and Eagle (2003, p. 272) and Diamond, Stovall-McClough, et al. (2003, p. 237) studied patients who had completed six months and twelve months of open-ended treatments of varied frequency, respectively. I would have difficulty forming an attachment to my therapist if I knew that the treatment would be ending in only twelve sessions. A six- to twelve-month interval of treatment seems like a reasonable time frame to expect that an attachment to the therapist would form.

Because the amount of time it takes to form an attachment to the therapist, and the factors that contribute to the time frame of an attachment, are both unknown, it would be important to study this phenomenon in its own right. Attachment research has traditionally focused on the quality of attachment rather than on the existence of an attachment (e.g., Ainsworth et al., 1978; Main et al., 1985). Recently, the assessment of the existence of an attachment has been studied in the adoption of Romanian orphans (Zeanah and Smyke, 2005). Parish and Eagle (2003, p. 277) assessed the strength of the attachment to the therapist rather than its quality per se and found that both the duration and frequency of treatment were positively correlated with most of their dimensional components of attachment to the therapist, including overall attachment. Attachment thresholds and factors that contribute to the rate of attachment formation were not studied, however.

The second issue I want to address is the validity of self-report measures of adult attachment. Researchers, working mostly from a social-psychology perspective, attempted to develop self-report instruments that yield assessments of internal working models of adult attachment (Bartholomew and Horowitz, 1991; Brennan, Clark, and Shaver, 1998; Collins and Read, 1990; Hazan and Shaver, 1987; Hindy and Schwarz, 1994; Simpson, 1990; Sperling and Berman, 1991; West, Sheldon, and Reiffer, 1987). In spite of their consistency with each other (Sperling, Foelsch, and Grace, 1996), self-report instruments nevertheless demonstrated little convergent validity with the AAI—the gold standard of adult attachment assessment (Bartholomew and Shaver, 1998; Crowell and Treboux, 1995; Crowell, Treboux, and Waters, 1999; de Haas, Bakermans-Kranenburg, and van IJzendoorn, 1994; Diamond et al., 1999; George and West, 1999; Main and Goldwyn, 1994; Roisman et al., 2007). This lack of correspondence is not surprising because self-report instruments measure conscious processes while the AAI "surprises"—and assesses—the unconscious (George, Kaplan, and Main, 1985, p. 6). Administering a self-report instrument rather than conducting an extensive, clinically informed interview regarding attachment relationships would be similar to handing a new patient a packet of questionnaires to complete in lieu of an initial in-depth consultation, and then expecting to derive equally reliable results.

Most crucially, these self-report instruments fail to detect the effects of defensive distortions on recall and narrative expression that reflect underlying distinctions in attachment organization (see also Dozier, 1990; Dozier and Lee, 1995; Dozier, Stevenson, Lee, and Velligan, 1991; Kobak and Sceery, 1988; Pianta, Egeland, and Adam, 1996; Shedler, Mayman, and Manis, 1993, 1994). Consistent with this explanation, Eagle (2006) has suggested that the concordance between self-report and narrative-based attachment items found by Westen and his colleagues (Westen et al., 2006) reflects the fact that an informant other than the patient (in this study, the therapist) completed their attachment instrument. The potential for self-deception among dismissing persons is especially great because of their need to maintain a grandiose self that underlies this attachment organization (Goodman, 2002).

Self-report instruments that purport to measure adult attachment also tend to focus on the quality of interpersonal relationships rather than on specific relationships on which a person relies during attachment-activating situations. These instruments are also unlikely to activate the attachment system during their administration. The AAI, on the other hand, was specifically designed to activate the attachment system to yield an accurate assessment of the person's internal working model by asking the interviewee to recall specific attachment-activating childhood events to support their general impressions of childhood relationships with their caregivers. An insufficiently stressed attachment system can yield inaccurate attachment classifications (e.g., Fonagy, Steele, and Steele, 1991; Goodman, Hans, and Cox, 1999). Thus, it is easy to understand the discrepancy between self-report instruments and narrative-based instruments coded by outside informants such as the AAI.

We would expect similar problems to plague the development of any instrument that purports to assess the patient's attachment to the therapist. Two of the three empirical approaches to assessing the patient's attachment to the therapist are self-report instruments, which would be vulnerable to the same flaws mentioned earlier in relation to self-report instruments of adult attachment. If these instruments are associated with so many threats to internal validity, then why do they seem so appealing? It has been suggested that the AAI—the gold standard of adult attachment assessment—is "time-consuming and complex to administer and is thus regarded as unsuitable for routine use" (Smallbone and Dodds, 2001, p. 32). Tedium would seem a small price to pay to achieve valid and reliable results. The consequence of taking a shortcut is that the results yielded by such instruments are difficult, perhaps even impossible, to interpret.

The three empirical approaches to assessing the patient's attachment to the therapist are (1) the Client Attachment to Therapist Scale (CATS; Mallinckrodt et al., 1995; Mallinckrodt et al., 1998; Mallinckrodt et al., 2005), (2) the Components of Attachment Questionnaire (CAQ; Parish and Eagle, 2003), and (3) the Patient-Therapist Adult Attachment Interview (PT-AAI; Diamond, Clarkin, et al., 2003; Diamond, Stovall-McClough, et al., 2003), formerly known as the Patient-Therapist Relationship Interview (Diamond et al., 1999). These three approaches all purport to measure the patient's attachment to the therapist but approach the task in different ways. Only one of these three instruments, the PT-AAI, uses a narrative-based assessment that resembles the AAI.

CLIENT ATTACHMENT TO THERAPIST SCALE (CATS)

The CATS is a thirty-six-item self-report measure of the patient's attachment to the therapist. In the initial study (Mallinckrodt et al., 1995), six psychologists and three psychology interns generated 143 items that they believed would measure some aspect of this construct. These items were pooled with 129 items the three authors themselves had generated to make 272 items. These items were then reduced to one hundred Likert-type items with six anchor points ranging from 1 (strongly disagree) to 6 (strongly agree). The authors used this version of the CATS to collect data on 138 outpatients at various agency- and university-based counseling centers and outpatient clinics. These outpatients completed the one-hundred-item CATS after a median of ten sessions. A Kaiser-Meyer-Olkin (KMO) measure of sampling adequacy was conducted, which reduced the item pool to seventy-five. Then a principal components analysis with oblique rotation was conducted in which all items that loaded greater than .40 on only a single factor were used to construct the three CATS subscales. The final item total was thirty-six, yielding three factors: secure (fourteen items), avoidant-fearful (twelve items), and preoccupied-merger (ten items). Internal consistencies of these subscales ranged from .63 to .81, and test-retest reliabilities on seventeen patients ranged from .72 to .86.

The secure subscale measures the extent to which the patient experiences the therapist as responsive, understanding, sensitive, and emotionally available. Further, the patient feels comforted by the therapist and encouraged to explore frightening or troubling mental content. The avoidant-fearful subscale measures the extent to which the patient experiences the therapist as disapproving, dishonest, and rejecting and thus feels reluctant to make self-disclosures. Further, the patient feels threatened, ashamed, or humiliated by the therapist. The preoccupied-merger subscale measures the extent to which the patient longs for increased therapist contact, wants to commit boundary violations with the therapist, and focuses on the therapist's personal life and other patients.

In this initial study, patients seen between five and eight sessions had lower secure scores than patients seen between nine and fifteen sessions. The authors (Mallinckrodt et al., 1995) suggested that either patients require more than eight sessions to form a secure attachment to their therapists, or patients with lower secure scores tend to drop out of treatment after eight sessions. Alternatively, perhaps these attachment security items begin to acquire meaning to patients only after eight sessions. For example, it would be difficult for a patient to respond meaningfully before only eight sessions to the item, "I feel sure that my counselor will be there if I really need her/him" (item 34; p. 311).

In addition, the CATS secure subscale was positively correlated with the CATS preoccupied-merger subscale and the three subscales (task, goal, and bond) of the WAI, negatively correlated with the CATS avoidant-fearful subscale and the four subscales (alienation, insecure attachment, egocentricity, and social incompetence) of the Bell Object Relations and Reality Testing Inventory (BORRTI), and uncorrelated with general self-efficacy and social self-efficacy (Mallinckrodt et al., 1995). By contrast, the CATS fearful-avoidant subscale was negatively correlated with the three subscales of the WAI, positively correlated with three of the four subscales of the BORRTI (not insecure attachment), and negatively correlated with general self-efficacy and social self-efficacy. The CATS preoccupied-merger subscale was uncorrelated with most of these criterion variables. Interestingly, none of the CATS subscales was correlated with the three subscales (depend, close, and anxiety) of the Adult Attachment Scale (AAS), a self-report instrument that purports to measure attachment in romantic relationships. The preoccupied-merger subscale was significantly correlated with the depend subscale of the AAS, but the effect size was modest ($r = .18$). In the abstract, the authors stated, "CATS factors correlated in expected directions with ... adult attachment" (p. 307), yet in the results, the authors acknowledged, "Correlations with the AAS subscales were less consistently supportive of CATS construct validity" (p. 312). Many of these correlations (located on p. 313) were not in the expected directions.

These correlations with the AAS are important because they would help to establish the construct validity of the CATS. Given the fact that attachment patterns with parents generalize to romantic partners (Feeney, 1999), it seems reasonable to assume that these same patterns would also generalize to attachment patterns with therapists. We would expect, therefore, that the correlations between the AAS and the CATS would be significant. If the therapist's vocal and behavioral communications also contribute to the quality of the patient's attachment to the therapist, then we would expect the correlations between the AAS and the CATS to be in the moderate range. Because none of the nine correlations among the six subscales of these two instruments was higher than $r = .18$, we need to question the construct validity of the AAS, the CATS, or both instruments. The positive correlation between the secure and preoccupied-merger subscales also suggests psychometric difficulties because we would theoretically expect these two subscales to be negatively correlated with each other.

Finally, the authors (Mallinckrodt et al., 1995) performed a cluster analysis with the three subscales and the WAI total scores, which yielded four clusters that they labeled "secure," "reluctant," "avoidant," and "merger." The reluctant cluster scored high on both the secure and avoidant-fearful subscales, which the authors interpreted as a reluctance to self-disclose to the therapist in spite of an overall feeling of security. Alternatively, they suggested that "a considerable degree of denial influenced these clients' self-ratings" (p. 315).

In their second study, Mallinckrodt and his colleagues (Mallinckrodt et al., 1998) collected data on sixty-one outpatients who had completed between nine and twenty therapy sessions ($M = 9.7$) and found that the CATS secure subscale was negatively correlated with alexithymia and fear of family separation. The avoidant-fearful subscale was positively correlated with alexithymia, fear of family separation, marital conflict, and parent-child role reversal. The preoccupied-merger subscale was positively correlated with alexithymia, fear of family separation, and marital conflict. These findings were expected; a patient who scores low on security is likely to experience family insecurity and difficulty expressing his or her feelings. Only parent-child role reversal was able to discriminate the two insecure CATS subscales (avoidant-fearful and preoccupied-merger).

In their final study, Mallinckrodt and his colleagues (Mallinckrodt et al., 2005) administered the CATS to thirty-eight patients in their fourth to eighth sessions out of a maximum of twelve sessions of therapy. The authors also administered the WAI, BORRTI, the two subscales (anxiety and avoidance) of the Experiences in Close Relationships Scale (ECRS), and the three subscales (depth, smoothness, and exploration) of the Session Evaluation Questionnaire (SEQ). The ECRS measures the patient's quality of attachment in romantic relationships, while the SEQ measures the patient's perception of the psychotherapy process. Depth measures the perceptions of the therapy session's value and power, while smoothness measures the perceptions of the therapy session's comfort, relaxation, and pleasantness. The exploration subscale consists of the sum of the depth and smoothness subscales. A therapy session that scores high on both depth and smoothness reflects "smooth sailing" (p. 87)—an optimal level of internal examination and sense of safety. A session that scores high on depth and low on smoothness reflects "heavy going" (p. 87)—such intense internal examination that the accompanying anxiety makes the session unproductive. A session that scores low on depth and high on smoothness reflects "coasting" (p. 87)—a superficial therapy experience with no mobilization of anxiety.

Mallinckrodt and his colleagues (Mallinckrodt et al., 2005) found that the CATS secure subscale was positively correlated with high depth, high smoothness, high exploration, and the three subscales of the WAI, highly negatively correlated with the CATS avoidant-fearful subscale ($r = -.68$), and uncorrelated with the CATS preoccupied-merger subscale and the ECRS anxiety and avoidance subscales. By contrast, the CATS avoidant-fearful subscale was positively correlated with the ECRS avoidance subscale; negatively correlated with high depth, high smoothness, high exploration, and the three subscales of the WAI; and uncorrelated with the CATS preoccupied-merger subscale. The CATS preoccupied-merger subscale was uncorrelated with all variables assessed. Because of the large effect size between the CATS secure and avoidant-fearful subscales and the lack of findings with the CATS preoccupied-merger subscale, it is plausible to suspect that the CATS secure and avoidant-fearful subscales measure opposite ends of one dimension—a security dimension. Considering also the equally large effect sizes between these two CATS subscales and the three subscales of the WAI ($r = .57-.69$), we could also wonder whether the CATS is simply a proxy for the WAI.

Mallinckrodt and his colleagues (Mallinckrodt et al., 2005) answered this question by testing whether the CATS could predict session exploration over and above the effects of the working alliance. Both the CATS secure and avoidant-fearful subscales predicted session exploration over and above the working alliance, while the working alliance did not predict session exploration over and above the two CATS subscales. The authors concluded that the CATS measures features of the patient's relationship with the therapist that do not overlap with the working alliance. Finally, another research group (Woodhouse et al., 2003) found that the CATS secure subscale was positively correlated with their therapists' ratings of their patients' negative transference in outpatient therapy of a median of ten months' duration. In other words, a patient's secure attachment to his or her therapist reflects a level of safety in this relationship that permits the emergence of negative affective reactions directed toward the therapist.

In summary, the CATS offers therapists a quick and easy method of assessing their patients' attachment to them. The CATS items have high face validity, and the instrument yields scores on three subscales that parallel known attachment categories. Moderate to large effect sizes with working alliance and object relations suggest some convergent validity with conceptually related constructs. The associations with session depth, smoothness, and exploration also suggest that the quality of the patient's attachment to the therapist affects the quality of psychotherapy process, or at least the patient's perceptions of this process. On the other hand, the CATS is mostly uncorrelated with self-report adult attachment constructs, the instruments with which we would expect the CATS to be most highly correlated. The intercorrelations among the three factors also suggest a single factor rather than three. That the CATS was administered after as few as four sessions raises the question whether the patients had sufficient time to form an attachment to the therapist. The self-report nature of the instrument also raises the possibility that certain patients (e.g., dismissing patients) could defensively inflate their CATS secure subscale scores and deflate their scores on the other two subscales. Finally, the therapist's contribution to the patient's attachment to him or her is not measured. Aware of this problem, Mallinckrodt and his colleagues (Mallinckrodt et al., 1995) remarked, "Therapists offer the relationship conditions that make an attachment possible, and it would be a serious mistake to attribute difficulty in establishing a secure psychotherapy attachment entirely to client factors" (p. 316). A measurement of the therapist's attachment history could contextualize the patient's CATS subscale scores and perhaps make them more interpretable.

COMPONENTS OF ATTACHMENT QUESTIONNAIRE (CAQ)

The CAQ is a forty-five-item self-report measure of the patient's attachment to the therapist. In the only published study (Parish and Eagle, 2003), a study group of advanced doctoral candidates conducting research on adult attachment generated items most relevant to nine components of attachment: proximity seeking, separation protest, secure base, safe haven, stronger/wiser, availability, strong feelings, particularity, and mental representation (see earlier discussion for brief descriptions of these components). Five items assess each of the nine components. The study group arrived at a consensus on all CAQ items. Two forms of the CAQ were constructed. One instrument, the CAQ-T, was designed to assess the patient's attachment to the therapist, while the other instrument, the CAQ-AF, was designed to assess the patient's attachment to a primary attachment figure (e.g., family member or partner). The forty-five Likert-type items of each questionnaire have five anchor points ranging from 1 (not at all true) to 5 (very true). The intensity of the patient's overall attachment to the therapist or primary attachment figure is calculated by taking the mean of all forty-five items. Each of the nine component scores is calculated by taking the mean of the five items that comprise that component. No factor analysis was conducted on these two instruments to derive attachment patterns like the CATS. No psychometric data were reported (e.g., internal consistency, test-retest reliability).

The authors (Parish and Eagle, 2003) used both versions of the CAQ to collect data on 105 patients participating in psychoanalysis or psychodynamic psychotherapy with the same therapist for a minimum of six months. Session frequency ranged from less than once per week to four times per week. Patients were recruited from the caseloads of doctoral candidates from several training programs, from a university counseling center staffed by doctoral candidates, and from doctoral candidates participating in their own therapy. These patients completed the CAQ-T on their therapist, the CAQ-AF on the person to whom they felt closest, the Relationship Questionnaire (RQ; a self-report instrument that purports to measure adult attachment), and the WAI. Patients scored the therapist significantly higher than the primary attachment figure on only two components—wiser/stronger and availability. This finding suggests that on most components of attachment, the intensity of attachment to the primary attachment figure exceeds that to the therapist.

The CAQ-T intensity of overall attachment was positively correlated with the duration and frequency of treatment, the RQ secure subscale, and the WAI total score, negatively correlated with the RQ dismissing subscale, and uncorrelated with the RQ fearful and preoccupied subscales. The CAQ-T attachment component safe haven was negatively correlated with the RQ fearful subscale. In a multiple regression analysis, the CAQ-T attachment components secure base and availability predicted the WAI total score over and above the intensity of overall attachment and the seven other components. In addition, the authors discovered that female patients in treatment with male therapists demonstrated higher scores on the CAQ-T intensity of overall attachment than the other three gender pairings.

In summary, the CAQ-T, like the CATS, offers therapists a quick and easy method of assessing their patients' attachment to them. Also like the CATS, the CAQ-T items have high face validity. Unlike the CATS, however, the CAQ-T measures the intensity of nine components of attachment to the therapist rather than patterns of attachment to the therapist. The gold standard assessment methods of attachment—the Strange Situation (Ainsworth et al., 1978) and AAI (Main et al., 1985)—assess patterns rather than intensity, because attachment theory assumes that the attachment to the primary caregiver is equally intense for all humans. A therapist, however, would not be considered a primary caregiver; thus, we would expect the intensity of the attachment to the therapist to be more variable than that to the primary caregiver. In a therapeutic context, therefore, it might make sense to assess the intensity of attachment.

That the CAQ-T does not also yield attachment patterns, however, makes it impossible to establish convergent validity with other measures of adult attachment because all the other measures assess patterns, not intensity. Therefore, the correlations between the CAQ-T and the RQ secure and dismissing subscales are difficult to interpret. The findings indicate that patients who experience higher levels of security in relationships are also likely to experience higher levels of intensity in overall attachment to their therapist. Conversely, patients who experience higher levels of dismissal in relationships are also likely to experience lower levels of intensity in overall attachment to their therapist. We know from skin conductance levels that dismissing persons experience marked increases when they recall experiences of separation, rejection, and threat from parents during the AAI (Dozier and Kobak, 1992; Roisman, Tsai, and Chiang, 2004). Even anxious-avoidant infants who appear undistressed during reunion episodes with the caregiver experience increased heart rates and cortisol levels (Spangler and Grossmann, 1993; Sroufe and Waters, 1977).

On the CAQ-T, dismissing persons reported lower levels of intensity of attachment to the therapist, perhaps because they need to deny the emotional vulnerability that such an attachment entails. Contrary to Kernberg (1986b), who argued that narcissistic personalities demonstrate a persistent absence of separation anxiety, I argued that these persons, who tend to have dismissing attachment patterns (Allen, Hauser, and Borman-Spurrell, 1996; Rosenstein and Horowitz, 1996), are in denial over their acute separation anxiety because its acknowledgment would make them appear too vulnerable—to themselves and to others (Goodman, 2002). Dismissing persons' self-deception regarding their intensity of attachment to the therapist underscores my earlier argument against self-report measures of attachment. Finally, as with the CATS, the therapist's contribution to the patient's attachment to him or her is not measured.

PATIENT-THERAPIST ADULT ATTACHMENT INTERVIEW (PT-AAI)

Unlike the CATS and CAQ-T, the PT-AAI (Diamond, Clarkin, et al., 2003; Diamond, Stovall-McClough, et al., 2003), formerly known as the Patient-Therapist Relationship Interview (Diamond et al., 1999), uses a narrative-based assessment that resembles the AAI to measure "patients' and therapists' states of mind with respect to attachment and reflective function in the therapeutic relationship" (Diamond, Stovall-McClough, et al., 2003, p. 233). According to the authors (Diamond, Stovall-McClough, et al., 2003), the PT-AAI is a semi-structured interview that consists of twenty-eight questions regarding the nature of the therapeutic relationship. These questions are designed to stimulate memories of specific incidents that characterize this relationship, including the patient's responses to attachment-activating situations such as separations and illness. The first sixteen questions were modified directly from the AAI, while the final twelve questions specifically explore the therapist-patient relationship.

The PT-AAI is audiotaped, transcribed verbatim, and scored in much the same way as the AAI (Main and Goldwyn, 1994). Initially (Diamond, Clarkin, et al., 2003), the PT-AAI yielded five attachment classifications—F (secure), E (preoccupied), Ds (dismissing), U (unresolved), and CC (cannot classify). In an article published later that same year (Diamond, Stovall-McClough, et al., 2003), however, the U classification was dropped because "[U] is not relevant for the patient-therapist attachment relationship" (p. 234). Perhaps the authors assumed that a patient would not be classified as unresolved with respect to loss, abuse, or other traumatic events in his or her relationship to the therapist. Some coding scales used to make the classifications were modified (Diamond, Stovall-McClough, et al., 2003). For example, the loving versus unloving scale, which assesses the degree to which the adult experienced his or her caregivers from childhood as loving, was modified to the liking versus not-liking scale to reflect the degree to which the patient experienced the therapist as concerned, caring, and warm. The authors do not discuss the effects of modifying AAI questions and coding scales on the PT-AAI's construct validity or reliability. Interrater and test-retest reliabilities of classifications were not reported.

The F (secure) classification reflects the patient's coherent picture of the therapeutic relationship and the use of the therapist as a secure base. The corresponding therapist classification reflects the therapist's coherent picture of the therapeutic relationship and the confidence in his or her ability to function as a secure base for the patient. The Ds (dismissing) classification reflects the patient's idealization or devaluation of the therapeutic relationship and assertions of independence from the therapist. The corresponding therapist classification reflects the therapist's uniformly positive picture of the therapeutic relationship or acknowledgment of difficulties with little emotional depth or involvement. The E (preoccupied) classification reflects the patient's confused, incoherent picture of the therapeutic relationship and a preoccupation with the therapist expressed through dramatic behaviors designed to elicit the therapist's care. The corresponding therapist classification reflects the therapist's overinvolvement with the therapeutic relationship and overconcern about the patient's progress. The CC (cannot classify) classification reflects evidence of two or more different attachment strategies (Ds and E) or dramatic changes in strategy during the patient's or therapist's PT-AAI (Diamond, Stovall-McClough, et al., 2003).

The PT-AAI is also used to assess the concept of reflective functioning (RF)—the ability to understand the mental states of oneself and others. The RF coding manual (Fonagy, Target, Steele, and Steele, 1998) is directly applied to the PT-AAI transcript. The RFS has eleven anchor points ranging from -1 (anti-reflective, bizarre, or inappropriate RF) to 9 (full awareness of important aspects of all protagonists within an interaction). Each PT-AAI transcript receives one RF score. Interrater and test-retest reliabilities of RF scores were not reported. Interestingly, the authors developed the PT-AAI to assess not only the patient's state of mind but also the therapist's state of mind with respect to attachment to the other member of the therapeutic dyad (Diamond, Stovall-McClough, et al., 2003). Administering the PT-AAI to both patients and therapists reflects the authors' awareness—based on attachment research—that it takes two persons interacting with each other to form an attachment relationship.

The authors reported their findings in three articles (Diamond et al., 1999; Diamond, Clarkin, et al., 2003; Diamond, Stovall-McClough, et al., 2003). The first article (Diamond et al., 1999) reported on two outpatients diagnosed with borderline personality disorder (BPD). The second article (Diamond, Clarkin, et al., 2003) reported on these same two patients and three additional patients with BPD. The third article (Diamond, Stovall-McClough, et al., 2003) reported on the same five patients from the second article and five additional patients with BPD. Thus, the PT-AAI attachment classifications and RF scores of ten patients with BPD were reported. These ten patients (and their therapists) were administered the PT-AAI after one year of open-ended transference focused psychotherapy (Clarkin, Yeomans, and Kernberg, 1999; Kernberg et al., 1989). Frequency of treatment was reported in the first study as twice per week. In addition, the AAI was administered at four months and one year, and the attachment classifications and RF scores of these interviews for the ten patients were also reported. The authors' reporting of all these data easily permitted independent analysis of their findings (see p. 84ff).

The ten patient PT-AAI classifications and twenty patient AAI classifications (ten at four months + ten at one year) reported by the authors (Diamond, Stovall-McClough, et al., 2003) included alternative classifications—secondary, tertiary, and, in four out of thirty cases, quaternary or quinary classifications (e.g., CC/Ds1/Ds2/E2/E3, where numerals denote subclassifications; see Main and Goldwyn, 1994). Examining the primary classifications, we notice that the concordance between the PT-AAI classifications and one-year AAI classifications is 40 percent and between the PT-AAI classifications and four-month AAI classifications is 30 percent. Yet the authors concluded, "In all but one case, the patients' attachment state of mind with respect to the therapist on the PT-AAI is concordant with one or more aspects of the attachment state of mind with respect to the parents on the AAI at 4 months and/or 1 year" (p. 240).

How do we understand this discrepancy? It appears that the authors examined concordances between all the PT-AAI alternative classifications and all the AAI alternative classifications ("one or more aspects") and found a very high concordance. Of course, when some patients have been assigned one primary and four alternative classifications, it drastically increases the likelihood of finding a concordance between the two instruments. I suspect that the authors wanted to establish convergent validity between the PT-AAI and the AAI by demonstrating a high concordance between the two instruments. Yet I wonder whether reporting such a high concordance diminishes the importance of the therapist's contributions to the patient's attachment to him or her. We would expect only a moderate concordance between a patient's PT-AAI and AAI classifications because the attachment histories of not only the patient but also the therapist influence the patient's attachment pattern to the therapist (see figure 3.1). Unfortunately, the authors did not pursue other methods of internal validation of their instrument.

The authors (Diamond, Stovall-McClough, et al., 2003) also found that the ten therapist PT-AAI classifications were all secure. The secure subclassifications spanned the entire range from F1 (dismissing features) to F5 (preoccupied features). Dozier and her colleagues (Tyrrell et al., 1999) found that secondary attachment strategies used by securely attached case managers moderated patient outcomes. Diamond and her colleagues, however, did not report the associations between the therapist PT-AAI secure subclassifications and the four patients who shifted from an unresolved or cannot classify status to an organized (F, Ds, E) status on the AAI between four months and one year (pp. 239, 241).

Visual inspection of the data indicates that a dismissing patient who shifted to secure on the AAI at twelve months had a therapist classified as F3 (prototypically secure—neither dismissing nor preoccupied). An unresolved patient with a secondary classification of preoccupied who shifted to secure on the AAI at twelve months had a therapist classified as F5 (preoccupied features). The other two—unresolved patients with a secondary classification of dismissing who shifted to dismissing on the AAI at twelve months—had therapists classified as F5. Thus, two patients shifted to an organized attachment status with therapists whose secondary attachment strategy was noncomplementary with their patients. The other two patients shifted to a secure attachment status—one with a therapist whose secondary attachment strategy was complementary with his or her patient, the other with a therapist who was prototypically secure. Additional data would be needed to support Dozier's complementarity hypothesis. I am suggesting that therapists' secure subclassifications on the PT-AAI need to be analyzed in relation to shifts in their patient's attachment status to determine therapists' moderating effects on their patients' attachment organization and whether noncomplementary secondary attachment strategies produce more shifts than complementary strategies.

The authors (Diamond, Stovall-McClough, et al., 2003) also reported on the ten patient PT-AAI RF scores and twenty patient AAI RF scores (ten at four months + ten at one year) as well as the ten therapist PT-AAI RF scores. I entered the data into SPSS® and performed my own calculations to complement the calculations reported in the article. The Pearson correlation between the patients' RF scores on the PT-AAI and AAI at twelve months was marginally significant, $r = .63$, $p = .05$. A paired samples t-test revealed no significant difference between the two variables, $t(9) = .98$, $p = .35$. These findings indicate that the RF used by patients to describe their childhood relationships with their caregivers at twelve months is positively correlated with and not significantly different from the RF used to describe their therapists at twelve months.

The Pearson correlation between the patients' RF scores on the AAI at four months and at twelve months was highly significant, $r = .93$, $p < .001$ (also reported by the authors). A paired samples t-test, however, revealed a highly significant difference between the two variables, $t(9) = -4.85$, $p = .001$. These findings indicate that the RF used by patients to describe their childhood relationships with their caregivers at four months is positively correlated with and significantly lower than the RF used to describe their caregivers at twelve months.

The Pearson correlation between the patients' RF scores on the AAI at four months and the PT-AAI at twelve months was not significant, $r = .48$, $p = .16$ (incorrectly reported by the authors). A paired samples t-test revealed no significant difference between the two variables, $t(9) = -1.30$, $p = .23$. These findings indicate that the RF used by patients to describe their childhood relationships with their caregivers at four months is neither significantly correlated with nor significantly different from the RF used to describe their therapists at twelve months.

Finally, the Pearson correlation between the patients' and therapists' RF scores on the PT-AAI at twelve months was not significant, $r = .11$, $p = .77$. A paired samples t-test revealed a significant difference between the two variables, $t(9) = -3.35$, $p = .009$. These findings indicate that the RF used by patients to describe the relationship with the therapist is not significantly correlated with but significantly lower than the RF used by therapists to describe the relationship with the patient.

These results are interesting because they demonstrate that significant positive change occurred in patients' RF on the AAI between four and twelve months, contrary to the authors' report that "the improvement [in RF] was somewhat minimal" (Diamond, Stovall-McClough, et al., 2003, p. 240). The lack of a significant positive correlation between the AAI at four months and the PT-AAI at twelve months could be spurious because of the likelihood of type II errors associated with a small sample size; nevertheless, it could also reflect a lag in RF change between the caregiver representations and the therapist representation. In other words, RF change in relation to the therapist representation might lag behind RF change in relation to the caregiver representations. Further study with a larger sample size could test my hypothesis.

RF changes could also be analyzed in the context of shifts in attachment organization.

As expected, therapists' RF scores on the PT-AAI were significantly higher than patients' RF scores on the same instrument; however, these two sets of scores were uncorrelated ($r = .11$). This result conflicts with the conclusion of the authors: "The therapist's and patient's capacities for reflective function are mutually and reciprocally influential" (Diamond, Stovall-McClough, et al., 2003, p. 254). They revealed that one therapist, who treated three of the ten patients, obtained highly variable PT-AAI RF scores of 3, 6, and 7, which they interpreted as having been influenced by each patient's RF. If their conclusion were true, however, then these two sets of ten RF scores (therapists' and patients') would be significantly positively correlated. The PT-AAI presents a snapshot of the therapist's use of RF to describe to an interviewer his or her relationship to a patient. It is an intriguing finding that a therapist's RF could vary so greatly outside the therapeutic setting. It is possible that specific countertransference reactions could hinder or even help the therapist's mentalizing process; however, the authors do not speculate what kinds of countertransference reactions or patient characteristics are involved (p. 242).

In reanalyzing the authors' data, I remembered that Fonagy and his colleagues (Fonagy et al., 1996; Fonagy et al., 1995) had found that higher levels of RF buffered traumatized patients from developing BPD. Mentalization evolved in humans because it helped us to predict others' behavior, especially those who might want to harm us (Fonagy et al., 2002). I wondered whether therapists might also buffer themselves from the effects of overwhelming traumatic material presented by traumatized patients by mentalizing the patient in as sophisticated and complex a manner as possible. To test this hypothesis, I divided the sample into two groups: (1) patients with a primary AAI classification at four or twelve months of unresolved or cannot classify—classifications almost exclusively related to traumatic events (Hesse, 1996; Hesse and Main, 1999; Main and Goldwyn, 1994; Main and Hesse, 1990)—and (2) patients with a primary AAI classification at four or twelve months of secure, preoccupied, or dismissing.

I found an intriguing pattern of results in this admittedly tiny sample. While the mean patient RF scores did not differ significantly between these two groups, $t(8) = -1.61$, $p = .15$, the mean *therapist* RF scores did differ significantly between the two groups, $t(8) = -2.88$, $p = .02$, $r = .71$, with the therapists of traumatized patients scoring significantly higher RF ($M = 6.43$) than the therapists of the other patients ($M = 4.17$). These data suggest that therapists working with traumatized patients, whose mental contents might feel overwhelming, summon a highly sophisticated and complex RF to protect themselves from feeling so overwhelmed. Confirmation of my hypothesis awaits data collection on a larger sample.

The authors (Diamond, Stovall-McClough, et al., 2003) suggested that therapists optimally adjust their RF to a level only modestly higher than that of their patients to catalyze patients' understanding of mental states without overwhelming them with too much sophistication and complexity. According to the authors, Vygotsky's (1978) zone of proximal development illustrates how "the analyst flexibly navigates being ahead of, with, or even occasionally behind the patient, depending on which position might best promote the patient's capacity for mentalization at any particular stage of treatment" (p. 254). Unfortunately, the authors present no transcript data that would demonstrate this process in a therapy session, which could test their plausible hypothesis. Given the data available, collected outside the therapy session, an equally plausible hypothesis is that RF varies according to the therapist's need to arm him- or herself against overwhelming traumatic material. At four months, Patient 7 obtained an AAI RF score of -1 (the lowest possible score), but at twelve months obtained a PT-AAI RF score of 3 (p. 242). This four-point jump in RF was the highest increase in the entire sample, yet the difference between the patient's and therapist's PT-AAI RF score at twelve months was 4—the largest difference in the entire sample. This therapist obviously did not adjust his RF to create a zone of proximal development for the patient's RF, yet the patient's RF growth of four points in eight months was enormous compared to the other nine patients ($M = .28$).

I am suggesting that this therapist cultivated a high RF in thinking about this patient to protect himself from this patient's overwhelming traumatic material. The authors (Diamond, Stovall-McClough, et al., 2003) reported that this patient described her mother as "alternately neglectful and abusive toward her" (p. 243) and ultimately died when the patient was age thirteen. The father abandoned the family when the patient was age three. The authors described this patient's personal history as "one of unrelenting loss, abuse, and neglect" (p. 243). Not surprisingly, the patient's behavior in sessions was erratic, seductive, and frightening: "[The patient] sometimes attempt[ed] to climb in the therapist's lap, undress him, or undress herself during session. On one occasion, she surreptitiously tried to cut herself in a session and then began beating her therapist on the chest with her fists when he tried to intervene" (p. 244).

We can easily understand why the therapist would need to summon an unusually sophisticated and complex RF (score = 7) to manage the overwhelming countertransference reactions he must have been experiencing with this patient. This phenomenon represents a therapist reaction to what Bion (1959) referred to as "attacks on linking." If the patient unconsciously uses the overwhelming traumatic material to attack the therapist's mentalizing (linking) function, then an experienced therapist would protect himself or herself by strengthening these links. This "supermentalizing" might be considered another facet of the principle of noncomplementarity discussed in chapters 2, 3, and 4 in which the therapist uses a high level of mentalizing to challenge the patient's anti-mentalizing stance.

I agree with Diamond and her colleagues that the therapist needs to *express* his or her mentalizing to the patient in a zone of proximal development *within* sessions to keep from baffling the patient. The width of this zone must depend on the valence of the transference, the phase of treatment, and situational events such as the therapist's illness, which could resonate with painful childhood events. The therapist's private mentalizing (resembling Bion's [1962] concept of reverie) *within and outside* sessions, however, should remain as sophisticated and complex as possible to protect the therapist from the patient's attacks on his or her mentalizing (linking). A low therapist PT-AAI RF score (e.g., RF = 3) suggests that the patient has successfully attacked the therapist's mentalizing process vis-à-vis his or her treatment and has possibly recapitulated the role of the caregiver from childhood who failed to hold the child in mind because of a similar mentalizing breakdown. Process data from psychotherapy transcripts could demonstrate the zone in which the therapist's moment-to-moment mentalizing operates and its effects on treatment outcome.

In summary, Diamond and her colleagues (Diamond, Clarkin, et al., 2003) concluded that the PT-AAI "functions as a measure of transference" (p. 170), yet the concordance between the patient AAI attachment classifications at four months and the PT-AAI attachment classifications at twelve months was only 30 percent, and the correlation between the two corresponding sets of RF scores was not significant. The authors also concluded that the PT-AAI "functions as a measure of therapeutic alliance" (p. 170). Unfortunately, measures of transference and therapeutic alliance were not administered to patients; therefore, no conclusions can be drawn about the PT-AAI's convergent validity with these constructs. Previously, I argued for the conceptual distinction among the working alliance, patient attachment to the therapist, and transference (see figure 3.1). A more modest claim—that the PT-AAI attempts to assess only the patient's attachment to the therapist—seems reasonable.

The idea that the PT-AAI assesses the therapist's attachment to the patient seems countertheoretical. The therapist does not seek comfort from the patient as a secure base or safe haven, nor does he or she perceive the patient as stronger or wiser. The patient should not be emotionally available or responsive to the therapist's attachment needs. In the therapist-patient relationship, it is not the attachment system that is activated in the therapist but rather the caregiving system (see figure 3.1). George and Solomon (1996, 1999) have found the caregiving system to be conceptually distinct from, yet associated with, the attachment system in caregivers; they have developed an instrument to assess the quality of the caregiving system in caregivers. Perhaps a similar instrument could be designed to assess the quality of the caregiving system in therapists. Thus, the patient PT-AAI has more face validity than the therapist PT-AAI.

Although the therapists in the study conducted by Diamond and her colleagues (Diamond, Stovall-McClough, et al., 2003) demonstrated no variability in PT-AAI attachment classification, their PT-AAI RF scores did vary within as well as among therapists. I suggested that the therapist's countertransference reaction toward overwhelming traumatic material influences the therapist's RF both within and outside sessions. Although not addressed by the authors, I also suspect that each therapist's baseline RF (perhaps assessed by the AAI) also influences their PT-AAI RF score. For example, a therapist's AAI RF score of 7 could represent the upper bound of the range of PT-AAI RF scores used to describe all their patients. Studies in which therapists demonstrate the courage to become research subjects and complete the AAI will help us to clarify the relations between therapists' and patients' AAI and PT-AAI RF scores. The therapist's mentalizing capacity both influences and is influenced by the patient's mentalizing capacity in nontrivial ways that include the patient's clinical material as well as the patient's and therapist's attachment histories and ongoing relationship with each other.

Even though its validity and reliability were not established, the patient version of the PT-AAI poses an advantage over the CATS and CAQ-T. The PT-AAI relies on narrative expression to assess the state of mind with respect to attachment rather than on self-report. Narrative expression reveals defensive distortions more easily than self-report measures because the interviewee is naïve to the PT-AAI coding system. An interviewee might claim that the therapist is wonderful, empathic, and genuine, yet fail to retrieve episodic memories to support these adjectives and thus fail at appearing securely attached to the therapist. As previously mentioned, dismissing persons can appear secure on self-report measures of attachment. Finally, the therapist version of the PT-AAI acknowledges the importance of the therapist's contribution to the patient's attachment to him or her; however, the nature of the therapist's relationship to the patient does not parallel the patient's relationship to the therapist, as this instrument suggests. A research group could instead design and administer an instrument that assesses the therapist's quality of caregiving of the patient. This idea would be consistent with my pathways model presented in figure 3.1. Future research could compare the patient PT-AAI with the CATS and CAQ-T to determine whether these three instruments are measuring the same constructs.

Chapter Six

Interaction Structures Formed by Therapist and Patient Secondary Attachment Strategies

> Anyone who hopes to learn the noble game of chess from books will soon discover that only the openings and end-games admit of an exhaustive systematic presentation and that the infinite variety of moves which develop after the opening defy any such description. This gap in instruction can only be filled by a diligent study of games fought out by masters. The rules which can be laid down for the practice of psycho-analytic treatment are subject to similar limitations.
>
> Sigmund Freud, "On Beginning the Treatment (Further Recommendations on the Technique of Psycho-analysis I)"

While Freud focused on the therapist's technical behaviors in characterizing the nature of clinical practice, the sparse literature on the role of attachment organization in therapist-patient relationships suggests that the attachment histories of both therapist and patient influence both the process and outcome of treatment (Bernier and Dozier, 2002; Bernier et al., 2005; Dozier, 2003; Dozier and Bates, 2004; Dozier et al., 1994; Dozier and Tyrrell, 1998; Tyrrell et al., 1999). Dozier and her colleagues have articulated the principle of noncomplementarity to characterize the optimal therapist-patient match vis-à-vis attachment (see chapter 3). Their research suggests that therapists are optimally effective with patients whose secondary attachment strategy differs from their own. Conversely, therapists are less effective with patients whose secondary attachment strategy resembles their own. These secondary strategies are patterns of emotion regulation and modes of relatedness to others based on attachment-activating experiences with caregivers from childhood.

In those situations in which the caregiver does not provide a secure base or safe haven, the child goes to "Plan B"—an alternative to the straightforward proximity-seeking and contact-maintaining behaviors that represent the hallmarks of secure attachment. Plan B comes in two varieties: deactivating and hyperactivating (Kobak et al., 1993). When proximity-seeking and contact-maintaining behaviors fail to deactivate the attachment system, the child can deactivate the attachment system by dismissing his or her attachment needs and avoid the caregiver. Adults who routinely use this secondary attachment strategy minimize, devalue, or dismiss the emotional importance of attachment relationships (Main and Goldwyn, 1994). The child can also hyperactivate the attachment system by exaggerating his or her attachment needs and expressing anger toward the caregiver. Adults who routinely use this secondary attachment strategy are angrily preoccupied with attachment relationships (Main and Goldwyn, 1994).

Although we would expect most therapists to have secure states of mind with respect to attachment (Diamond, Stovall-McClough, et al., 2003; Tyrrell et al., 1999), either by virtue of having had emotionally responsive caregivers or a long-term, intensive psychotherapy where a corrective emotional experience could occur, most of us do rely on a secondary attachment strategy when the primary strategy fails. For secure adults, these secondary attachment strategies are partially captured in the AAI secure subclassifications (Main and Goldwyn, 1994), which range from F1 (somewhat restricting or setting aside of attachment) to F5 (somewhat resentful or preoccupied with attachment). Wherever we as therapists lie on this deactivating-hyperactivating continuum partially determines how we regulate our emotional lives and relate to others (Kobak et al., 1993; Slade, 1999). Patients also use these secondary attachment strategies. Dismissing patients use the deactivating strategy, while preoccupied patients use the hyperactivating strategy.

I am proposing a 2 × 2 typology of interaction structures formed by these therapist and patient secondary attachment strategies (see figure 6.1). Four possible cells exist: deactivating therapists paired with deactivating patients (cell 1), hyperactivating therapists paired with deactivating patients (cell 2), deactivating therapists paired with hyperactivating patients (cell 3), and hyperactivating therapists paired with hyperactivating patients (cell 4). Psychoanalysts from the relational school (e.g., J. Greenberg, 2001a; I. Z. Hoffman, 1994; Kantrowitz, 2001) have argued in favor of the uniqueness of the therapist-patient relationship, which has been compared to "a snowflake" in which "no two are alike" (Kantrowitz, 2001, p. 403). If the therapist-patient relationship is unique, then it follows that the processes that facilitate therapeutic change would also vary from relationship to relationship. Nevertheless, just as

	Therapist	
Patient	Deactivating Dismissing (Ds)	Hyperactivating Preoccupied (E)
Deactivating Dismissing (Ds)	(1) Sterile (complementary): low depth, high smoothness, low arousal, rigid boundaries, overdifferentiation, overregulated affect	(2) Expressive (noncomplementary): high depth, high smoothness, moderate arousal, flexible boundaries, optimal differentiation, expressed affect
Hyperactivating Preoccupied (E)	(3) Containing (noncomplementary): high depth, high smoothness, moderate arousal, firm boundaries, optimal differentiation, contained affect	(4) Chaotic (complementary): high depth, low smoothness, high arousal, loose boundaries, undifferentiation, underregulated affect

Figure 6.1. Typology Presenting Four Interaction Structures Based on the Secondary Attachment Strategies of Therapist and Patient

every snowflake has six sides, so too does every therapist-patient relationship have a particular shape. In fact, I am proposing that every therapist-patient relationship can have four possible shapes. Specifying a range of shapes can help us also to specify a range of clinical interventions that accompany each of these shapes. I have not conceptualized these four broadly defined shapes to minimize the uniqueness of the therapist-patient relationship but rather to delineate patterns within the uniqueness that could facilitate the development of broadly defined technical principles that therapists could use beyond a single case.

I will divide the four cells into two groups: complementary interaction structures and noncomplementary interaction structures. Complementary interaction structures are patterns of therapist-patient interaction in which the therapist and patient match on their secondary attachment strategy (cells 1 and 4; see figure 6.1). Conversely, noncomplementary interaction structures are patterns of therapist-patient interaction in which the therapist and patient do not match on their secondary attachment strategy (cells 2 and 3; see figure 6.1). Dozier and her colleagues (Bernier and Dozier, 2002; Bernier et al., 2005; Dozier, 2003; Dozier and Bates, 2004; Dozier et al., 1994; Dozier and Tyrrell, 1998; Tyrrell et al., 1999) have suggested that noncomplementary matches are more therapeutically effective than complementary matches. I have incorporated this idea into my typology of therapist-patient interaction structures. My descriptions of these four interaction structures are necessarily caricatured to increase their heuristic value; however, from my experience as a therapist, clinical supervisor, and psychotherapy process researcher, therapist-patient relationships that broadly resemble the ones depicted below actually exist.

STERILE INTERACTION STRUCTURE (CELL 1): DEACTIVATING THERAPIST AND PATIENT

This complementary interaction structure formed by a therapist and a patient who both tend to use a deactivating strategy in their affect regulation and mode of relatedness is characterized by a sterile, lifeless treatment in which both partners avoid intense emotions and deeply conflictual issues. The low arousal level (see Allen, 2003) observed in these sessions reflects a low level of depth coupled with a high level of smoothness (see chapter 5)—what Mallinckrodt and his colleagues (Mallinckrodt et al., 2005) might call "coasting" (p. 87). The consequence is a superficial therapy experience with little mobilization of anxiety and minimal personality change. McBride and her colleagues (McBride et al., 2006) found that deactivating patients paired with CBT treatment for depression (a treatment that deemphasizes interpersonal connections) experienced greater symptom relief than deactivating patients paired with IPT treatment for depression (a treatment that emphasizes interpersonal connections). Previously, I argued that the matching of deactivating patients with CBT is a complementary correspondence because this kind of treatment does not challenge the patient's deactivating strategy. Symptom relief occurred because this treatment merely strengthened failing defenses rather than produced lasting personality change (Eagle, 2006). Similarly, a sterile interaction structure strengthens the patient's defensive processes and never challenges the denial of attachment needs and vulnerability consistent with a false self (Winnicott, 1960).

Another feature of a sterile interaction structure is an air of formality in which the therapist maintains rigid boundaries and permits long silences. The therapist does not perceive him or herself as a caregiver per se but rather perhaps as a surgeon excising a tumor. There is a palpable lack of warmth or affection between the two partners, who seem invested in maintaining the status quo. The therapist or patient might be late to sessions without exploration of its potential meanings. The therapist or patient might also cancel sessions at the last minute and generally behave in a rejecting manner toward each other because each partner deactivates his or her needs. The patient denies his or her attachment needs and ignores any anxiety associated with vacations and other separations from the therapist; the therapist denies his or her caregiving needs and ignores any subtle patient cues that might suggest vulnerability associated with attachment to the therapist. For example, the patient arrives fifteen minutes late to a session immediately following a weeklong therapist vacation. The therapist ignores the patient's lateness as a cue that the separation had been unconsciously upsetting to the patient. By not exploring the patient's feelings, the therapist confirms the patient's expectations that others are rejecting of his or her attachment needs and that interdependent relationships are unimportant, overvalued, or nonexistent. Thus, the patient defensively excludes these needs as he or she did throughout childhood. I suspect that this interaction structure produces a high dropout rate.

CHAOTIC INTERACTION STRUCTURE (CELL 4): HYPERACTIVATING THERAPIST AND PATIENT

This complementary interaction structure formed by a therapist and a patient who both tend to use a hyperactivating strategy in their affect regulation and mode of relatedness is characterized by a chaotic, entangled treatment in which both partners rely on each other for support in an intensely emotional climate. The high arousal level (see Allen, 2003) observed in these sessions reflects a high level of depth coupled with a low level of smoothness—what Mallinckrodt and his colleagues (Mallinckrodt et al., 2005) might call "heavy going" (p. 87). The consequence is an intense, overstimulating, enmeshed therapy experience with high mobilization of anxiety and minimal personality change. The therapist and patient engage in mutual caregiving, thus reducing the role distinctions between the two partners.

Another feature of a chaotic interaction structure is an air of informality in which the therapist maintains loose boundaries, makes frequent self-disclosures, and talks incessantly. The therapist perceives him or herself alternately as a caregiver and as a child, who feels overwhelmed by the patient's material and sometimes looks to the patient for comfort. The sessions contain high emotional content that might include physical affection as well as arguments and occasional cold silences between the two partners. The therapist reacts reflexively to the patient's material rather than reflecting on it. Mirroring of the patient's needs lacks differentiation and marking (Fonagy et al., 2002; Gergely, 2000). For example, the patient discloses that her physician has scheduled her for a breast biopsy, which makes her feel terrified. The patient wants the therapist to sit closer to her in session and wants to talk to the therapist later that evening if the panicky feelings persist. The therapist gives her his home telephone number, sits next to her, and discloses that he too feels terrified about it. The therapist fails to contain the patient's anxiety and provide an experience of marking in which the patient senses that the therapist understands her terrified feelings but also feels something else (e.g., reassured that a biopsy is not the equivalent of having cancer). By feeling overwhelmed by the patient's feelings, the therapist confirms the patient's expectations that others are too fragile and undependable to contain attachment anxiety; therefore, the patient continues to feel fragmented. I suspect that this interaction structure might persist because the patient feels too vulnerable to leave treatment.

EXPRESSIVE INTERACTION STRUCTURE (CELL 2): HYPERACTIVATING THERAPIST AND DEACTIVATING PATIENT

This noncomplementary interaction structure, formed by a therapist who tends to use a hyperactivating strategy and a patient who tends to use a deactivating strategy in their affect regulation and mode of relatedness, is characterized by an expressive treatment in which the therapist helps the patient to express his or her needs, particularly attachment needs, as well as general feelings of vulnerability. The moderate arousal level (see Allen, 2003) observed in these sessions reflects a high level of depth coupled with a high level of smoothness—what Mallinckrodt and his colleagues (Mallinckrodt et al., 2005) might call "smooth sailing" (p. 87). The consequence is a gentle exploration of vulnerability with optimal mobilization of anxiety and the potential for personality change. This interaction structure gently challenges the patient's defensive processes, especially the denial of attachment needs and vulnerability consistent with a false self (Winnicott, 1960).

Another feature of an expressive interaction structure is the establishment of flexible boundaries that challenge the patient's rigid invulnerability. The therapist balances silences with affect-focused conversation that increases the patient's awareness of the therapist's recognition of attachment needs as a legitimate and valuable part of relating to others. The therapist perceives him or herself as a responsive caregiver trying to connect emotionally with a young child who miscues (see Cooper et al., 2005, p. 136) independence and self-sufficiency but whose underlying needs signal for security and closeness. Marking consists of acknowledging the patient's perception of a lack of attachment needs but also expressing the absent feelings on behalf of the patient. This marking creates a differentiated third point between therapist and patient that facilitates mentalization and affect regulation (Aron, 2006). The therapist inquires about the patient's lateness or missed appointments and explores feelings related to vacations and other separations even though the patient might dismiss his or her feelings about these events. The therapist also demonstrates an openness, warmth, and affection for the patient even though the patient ignores or avoids these experiences. As often as possible, the therapist needs to disconfirm the patient's expectations that others are rejecting of attachment needs and that interdependent relationships are unimportant, overvalued, or nonexistent.

I am treating a seventeen-year-old boy with Asperger's disorder whose parents forced him to enter therapy because he had become belligerent with his mother. As we might expect, I found him to be extraordinarily difficult to establish a rapport with, not only because of his illness but also because his parents forced him into therapy. I felt chronically rejected by him in sessions. He often said, "I don't want to be here; this is a waste of time." Long silences sometimes filled the space between us. When I asked him what he would normally be doing at 12:45 p.m. on a Saturday afternoon, he replied, "Sleeping." Gradually, I was able to develop enough of a working alliance to get him to tell me what was going on between his mother and him. I learned that his mother is a chronic alcoholic who behaves erratically around him and denigrates him when she is intoxicated. I also wondered whether she might have untreated bipolar disorder. I fought through my negative countertransference reactions and kept reaching out to him even though he kept rejecting me. Recently, he has begun to open up to me about his long-term goals, which include college and living on his own. When I do not see him for two weeks, I always inquire how he felt about the missed session even though I know the answer will always be, "I got to sleep in last weekend." I suspect that this expressive interaction structure will keep him in therapy because I am encouraging him—and permitting him—to express feelings of vulnerability, which he is beginning to value.

CONTAINING INTERACTION STRUCTURE (CELL 3): DEACTIVATING THERAPIST AND HYPERACTIVATING PATIENT

This noncomplementary interaction structure, formed by a therapist who tends to use a deactivating strategy and a patient who tends to use a hyperactivating strategy in their affect regulation and mode of relatedness, is characterized by a containing (Bion, 1962, p. 102) treatment in which the therapist helps the patient to contain his or her affects and thus facilitates their regulation. Like the expressive interaction structure, the moderate arousal level (see Allen, 2003) observed in these sessions reflects a high level of depth coupled with a high level of smoothness—"smooth sailing" (Mallinckrodt et al., 2005, p. 87). The consequence is a gentle, reflective, nonreactive exploration with optimal mobilization of anxiety and the potential for personality change. This interaction structure gently challenges the patient's affect dysregulation by facilitating mutual dyadic regulation.

Another feature of a containing interaction structure is the establishment of firm boundaries that challenge the patient's desire for an undifferentiated experience with the therapist. The therapist balances silences with clarifications, confrontations, and interpretations in the context of the patient's affect dysregulation, especially within the therapist-patient relationship. The therapist labels self- and object representations and the affects linking them to provide an integrative experience and thereby facilitate affect regulation. This process will help the patient build internal structure and diminish his or her experience of fragmentation. The therapist perceives him or herself as a responsive caregiver trying to contain the distress of a young child who "miscues" (see Cooper et al., 2005, p. 136) dependence and clinging but whose underlying needs signal for exploration and differentiation. Marking consists of acknowledging the patient's perception of distress but also communicating through a calm demeanor that the patient, like the child, "is not dying and will get over it" (Aron, 2006, p. 358). This marking creates a differentiated third point between therapist and patient that facilitates mentalization and affect regulation (Aron, 2006). The therapist listens to and absorbs the patient's anger related to vacations and other separations, and responds with an emotional reserve that communicates to the patient that the intensity of distress is not proportionate to the event. As often as possible, the therapist needs to disconfirm the patient's expectations that others are too fragile and undependable to contain attachment anxiety.

I treated an inpatient woman diagnosed with BPD who yelled at me for almost an entire forty-five-minute session after I had returned from a one-week vacation. I bided my time, listening and waiting for the storm to pass. In the next session, we were able to process her reaction to my absence without the affect dysregulation that accompanied the session that had immediately followed my return. I could identify with her feelings of longing and frustration, but my calm demeanor suggested that my emotional response was differentiated from hers. My initial countertransference reaction was to defend myself, and I fantasized saying something like "Don't I have a right to get away from you every once in a while?" I fought through my countertransference reaction and stayed calm long enough to allow myself to be a container for her rage. Over time, these accumulated experiences of containment helped her to realize that her rage was not toxic, as she had thought. I disappointed her at times, but my emotional availability was "good enough" (Winnicott, 1965, p. 57) to allow her to modulate her own emotional reactions to ungratified attachment needs and to increase her awareness of simultaneous needs for differentiation and autonomy. I suspect that this containing interaction structure kept my patient from leaving the hospital against medical advice (which she had considered) because she experienced relief that I had survived the negative transference without collapsing or retaliating (Casement, 2001). She can become a separate person without either one of us dying.

The four interaction structures I have outlined—sterile, chaotic, expressive, and containing—are, of course, caricatures of therapy sessions conducted by fictitious therapists and patients, each of whom falls on one of two ends of a continuum of secondary attachment strategies that range from deactivating to hyperactivating (Kobak et al., 1993, p. 235). Ideally, a therapist is sufficiently secure and flexible in his or her attachment organization that he or she can challenge whatever strategy a patient presents with by adopting a noncomplementary strategy to provide a corrective emotional experience for the patient (Alexander and French, 1946). A therapist who tends to use a hyperactivating strategy must behave in a slightly deactivating manner with a hyperactivating patient to produce effective personality change, not only in declarative symbolic knowledge but also in implicit procedural knowledge. Conversely, a therapist who tends to use a deactivating strategy must behave in a slightly hyperactivating manner with a deactivating patient to produce effective personality change. Researchers could assign therapists and patients randomly to these four cells to verify the principle of noncomplementarity (Bernier and Dozier, 2002; Bernier et al., 2005; Dozier, 2003; Dozier and Bates, 2004; Dozier et al., 1994; Dozier and Tyrrell, 1998; Tyrrell et al., 1999). Clinical training programs could assess the attachment organization of trainees (and their supervisors) and patients and use this information to help trainees learn how to provide noncomplementary psychotherapy experiences for their patients. However instructive these four broadly outlined interaction structures might be for the conduct of and training in psychotherapy, they can never substitute for the unique shape of each individual therapist-patient relationship.

Afterword

> An analytic treatment is like a snowflake. Overall, it is easy to identify and distinguish. However, closer scrutiny reveals how different each one is from the others. In fact, no two are alike. Nor are any two patient-analyst pairs. In analytic treatment, the particular aspects of therapeutic action that facilitate psychological change are likely to vary from person to person.
>
> Kantrowitz, 2001, p. 403

In this book, we have taken the inexorable journey from Freud and his one-person psychology to a pluralistic therapeutic voice and a two-person psychology. In some quarters, however, contemporary psychotherapy is urging the field to return to an earlier stop on this journey by manualizing the therapeutic encounter. By turning this creative, dynamic interaction into a set of procedures to be rigidly followed, contemporary psychotherapy deprives itself of its healing force. We lay down our knowledge, our wisdom, our clinical intuition, and put on our chef's hat, eager to follow the recipes already written out for us.

I want to make a plea for a measure of flexibility in the treatment of our patients. Despite diagnostic similarities, patients' needs and responses to therapeutic interventions vary widely. To meet these diverse needs, therapists need to implement intervention strategies tailored to the unique characteristics of each patient rather than boilerplate strategies designed for every patient. Therapeutically effective therapists adjust their technical approaches "on the fly" when they feel that their patients can benefit from a change in their intervention strategies. These technical modifications do not come from a treatment manual but from clinical intuition—the reflection on one's own countertransference reactions, or possibly a more broadly conceptualized empathic connection with the patient.

Specifically, treatments of patients with various levels of disturbance or different constellations of symptoms, treatments in various settings (e.g., inpatient, day treatment, outpatient), and treatments that systematically take advantage of pairings of therapist and patient attachment organizations are beginning to yield findings in which adherence to particular therapeutic modalities varies according to "conditions on the ground," to borrow a currently popular political phrase. Slavish adherence to a training manual can spell disaster, as Castonguay and his colleagues (Castonguay, Goldfried, Wiser, Raue, and Hayes, 1996) learned. While taking this inexorable journey, we have discovered an important clinical reality: treatment purity (whether psychoanalysis or CBT) might not be most effective for certain types of patients. Our students need to be empathically attuned to their patients' unique treatment needs so that they can become aware when their treatment approach becomes counterproductive. Training in global clinical skills such as empathy, countertransference awareness, and potential interaction structures (i.e., enactments) would more suitably position our students to become effective therapists than training them how to apply a treatment manual. Instead of training our students to be slaves to a treatment manual, we should be training them to be its master. Our field needs fewer technicians and more artists.

Finally, teaching therapist adherence to two or three broad treatment approaches (e.g., psychodynamic therapy and CBT) should become a vital aspect of clinical training; however, teaching therapist adherence to narrowly focused treatment manuals such as bedtime noncompliance (Ferber, 2006) ensnares our field in the "narcissism of minor differences" (Freud, 1918, p. 199) and immerses our students in memorizing procedures rather than experiencing relationships. The endless proliferation of manualized psychotherapies that emphasize their uniqueness obscures the broadly conceptualized therapeutic processes common to all effective psychotherapies. Psychotherapy process researchers need to focus on the common therapeutic ingredients of all effective psychotherapies and organize under a unified banner rather than splinter the field by promoting one's own treatment approach. Examining therapeutic processes that actually work moves us "beyond brand names" and inevitable sectarian strife and instead unites us in a common objective—to help relieve patients of their suffering.

References

Ainsworth, M. D. S. (1979). Infant-mother attachment. *American Psychologist, 34*, 932–37.

Ainsworth, M. D. S., Bell, S. M., & Stayton, D. J. (1974). Infant-mother attachment and social development: "Socialization" as a product of reciprocal responsiveness to signals. In M. P. M. Richards (Ed.), *The integration of a child into a social world* (pp. 99–135). Cambridge: Cambridge University Press.

Ainsworth, M. D. S., Blehar, M. C., Waters, E., & Wall, S. (1978). *Patterns of attachment: A psychological study of the strange situation.* Hillsdale, NJ: Erlbaum.

Alexander, F., & French, T. M. (1946). *Psychoanalytic therapy: Principles and application.* Oxford: Ronald.

Allen, J. G. (2003). Mentalizing. *Bulletin of the Menninger Clinic, 67*, 91–112.

Allen, J. P., Hauser, S. T., & Borman-Spurrell, E. (1996). Attachment theory as a framework for understanding sequelae of severe adolescent psychopathology: An 11-year follow-up study. *Journal of Consulting and Clinical Psychology, 64*, 254–63.

Altman, N., Briggs, R., Frankel, J., Gensler, D., & Pantone, P. (2002). *Relational child psychotherapy.* New York: Other Press.

American Psychiatric Association. (2000). *Diagnostic and statistical manual of mental disorders* (Fourth ed., text revision). Washington, DC: Author.

Amini, F., Lewis, T., Lannon, R., Louie, A., Baumbacher, G., McGuinness, T., & Schiff, E. Z. (1996). Affect, attachment and memory: Contributions toward psychobiologic integration. *Psychiatry, 59*, 213–39.

Arizmendi, T., Beutler, L., Shanfield, S., Crago, M., & Hagaman, R. (1985). Client-therapist value similarity and psychotherapy outcome: A microscopic analysis. *Psychotherapy, 22*, 16–21.

Aron, L. (2006). Analytic impasse and the third: Clinical implications of intersubjectivity theory. *International Journal of Psycho-Analysis, 87*, 349–68.

Bartholomew, K., & Horowitz, L. M. (1991). Attachment styles among young adults: A test of a four-category model. *Journal of Personality and Social Psychology, 61*, 226–44.

Bartholomew. K., & Shaver, P. R. (1998). Methods of assessing adult attachment: Do they converge? In J. A. Simpson and W. S. Rholes (Eds.), *Attachment theory and close relationships* (pp. 25–45). New York: Guilford Press.

Beck, A. T. (1976). *Cognitive therapy and the emotional disorders*. New York: International Universities Press.

Benjamin, J. (1987). The decline of the Oedipus complex. In J. M. Broughton (Ed.), *Critical theories of psychological development* (pp. 211–44). New York: Plenum Press.

———. (2002). The rhythm of recognition: Comments on the work of Louis Sander. *Psychoanalytic Dialogues, 12*, 43–53.

———. (2004). Beyond doer and done to: An intersubjective view of thirdness. *Psychoanalytic Quarterly, 73*, 5–46.

Bernier, A., & Dozier, M. (2002). The client-counselor match and the corrective emotional experience: Evidence from interpersonal and attachment research. *Psychotherapy: Theory/Research/Practice/Training, 39*, 32–43.

Bernier, A., Larose, S., & Soucy, N. (2005). Academic mentoring in college: The interactive role of student's and mentor's interpersonal dispositions. *Research in Higher Education, 46*, 29–51.

Berzins, J. I. (1977). Therapist-patient matching. In A. S. Gurman and A. M. Razin (Eds.), *Effective psychotherapy: A handbook of research* (pp. 222–51). New York: Pergamon Press.

Beutler, L. E. (1991). Have all won and must all have prizes? Revisiting Luborsky et al.'s verdict. *Journal of Consulting and Clinical Psychology, 59*, 226–32.

Beutler, L. E., Clarkin, J. F., Crago, M., & Bergan, J. (1991). Client-therapist matching. In C. R. Snyder and D. R. Forsyth (Eds.), *Handbook of social and clinical psychology: The health perspective* (pp. 699–716). New York: Pergamon Press.

Beutler, L. E., Crago, M., & Arizmendi, T. G. (1986). Therapist variables in psychotherapy process and outcome. In S. L. Garfield and A. E. Bergin (Eds.), *Handbook of psychotherapy and behavior change* (Third ed., pp. 257–310). New York: Wiley.

Beutler, L. E., Pollack, S., & Jobe, A. M. (1978). "Acceptance," values, and therapeutic change. *Journal of Consulting and Clinical Psychology, 46*, 198–99.

Bion, W. R. (1959). Attacks on linking. *International Journal of Psycho-Analysis, 40*, 308–15.

———. (1962). *Learning from experience*. London: Heinemann.

———. (1967). *Second thoughts*. London: Heinemann.

Bishop, S. R., Lau, M., Shapiro, S., Carlson, L., Anderson, N. D., Carmody, J., Segal, Z. V., Abbey, S., Speca, M., Velting, D., & Devins, G. (2004). Mindfulness: A proposed operational definition. *Clinical Psychology: Science and Practice, 11*, 230–41.

Bordin, E. S. (1994). Theory and research on the therapeutic working alliance: New directions. In A. O. Horvath and L. S. Greenberg (Eds.), *The working alliance: Theory, research, and practice* (pp. 13–37). New York: Wiley.

Bowlby, J. (1958). The nature of the child's tie to his mother. *International Journal of Psycho-Analysis, 39*, 350–73.

———. (1973). *Attachment and loss: Vol. 2. Separation: Anxiety and anger*. New York: Basic Books.

———. (1977a). The making and breaking of affectional bonds. I. Aetiology and psychopathology in the light of attachment theory. *British Journal of Psychiatry, 130,* 201–10.

———. (1977b). The making and breaking of affectional bonds: II. Some principles of psychotherapy. *British Journal of Psychiatry, 130,* 421–31.

———. (1980). *Attachment and loss: Vol. 3. Loss, sadness and depression.* New York: Basic Books.

———. (1982). *Attachment and loss: Vol. 1. Attachment* (Second ed.). New York: Basic Books.

———. (1988). *A secure base: Parent-child attachment and healthy human development.* New York: Basic Books.

Bradley, R., Heim, A. K., & Westen, D. (2005). Transference patterns in the psychotherapy of personality disorders: Empirical investigation. *British Journal of Psychiatry, 186,* 342–49.

Brennan, K. A., Clark, C. L., & Shaver, P. R. (1998). Self-report measurement of adult attachment: An integrative overview. In J. A. Simpson and W. S. Rholes (Eds.), *Attachment theory and close relationships* (pp. 46–76). New York: Guilford Press.

Britton, R. (1998). *Belief and imagination: Exploration in psychoanalysis.* London: Tavistock/Routledge.

Burns, P., Sander, L. W., Stechler, G., & Julia, H. (1972). Distress in feeding: Short-term effects of caretaker environment of the first 10 days. *Journal of the American Academy of Child Psychiatry, 11,* 427–39.

Casement, P. J. (2001). The analyst's participation: A new look [Commentary]. *Journal of the American Psychoanalytic Association, 49,* 381–86.

Cassidy, J., & Kobak, R. R. (1988). Avoidance and its relation to other defensive processes. In J. Belsky and T. Nezworski (Eds.), *Clinical implications of attachment* (pp. 300–323). Hillsdale, NJ: Erlbaum.

Cassidy, J., Woodhouse, S. S., Cooper, G., Hoffman, K., Powell, B., & Rodenberg, M. (2005). Examination of the precursors of infant attachment security: Implications for early intervention and intervention research. In L. J. Berlin, Y. Ziv, L. Amaya-Jackson, and M. T. Greenberg (Eds.), *Enhancing early attachments: Theory, research, intervention, and policy* (pp. 34–60). New York: Guilford Press.

Castonguay, L. G., Goldfried, M. R., Wiser, S., Raue, P. J., & Hayes, A. M. (1996). Predicting the effect of cognitive therapy for depression: A study of unique and common factors. *Journal of Consulting and Clinical Psychology, 64,* pp. 497–504.

Charone, J. K. (1981). Patient and therapist treatment goals related to psychotherapy outcome (Doctoral dissertation, Yeshiva University, 1981). *Dissertation Abstracts International, 42*(1-B), 365.

Clark, R. W. (1980). *Freud: The man and the cause.* New York: Random House.

Clarkin, J. F., Yeomans, F. E., & Kernberg, O. F. (1999). *Psychotherapy for borderline personality.* New York: Wiley.

Collins, N. L., & Read, S. J. (1990). Adult attachment, working models, and relationship quality in dating couples. *Journal of Personality and Social Psychology, 58,* 644–63.

Cooper, G., Hoffman, K., Powell, B., & Marvin, R. (2005). The Circle of Security intervention: Differential diagnosis and differential treatment. In L. J. Berlin, Y. Ziv, L.

Amaya-Jackson, and M. T. Greenberg (Eds.), *Enhancing early attachments: Theory, research, intervention, and policy* (pp. 127–51). New York: Guilford Press.

Craighead, W. E., Sheets, E. S., Bjornsson, A. S., & Arnarson, E. O. (2005). Specificity and nonspecificity in psychotherapy. *Clinical Psychology: Science and Practice, 12*, 189–93.

Crastnopol, M. (2001). The analyst's participation: A new look [Commentary]. *Journal of the American Psychoanalytic Association, 49*, 386–98.

Crowell, J. A., & Treboux, D. (1995). A review of adult attachment measures: Implications for theory and research. *Social Development, 4*, 294–327.

Crowell, J. A., Treboux, D., & Waters, E. (1999). The Adult Attachment Interview and the Relationship Questionnaire: Relations to reports of mothers and partners. *Personal Relationships, 6*, 1–18.

Curhan, J. R., & Pentland, A. (2007). Thin slices of negotiation: Predicting outcomes from conversational dynamics within the first 5 minutes. *Journal of Applied Psychology, 92*, 802–11.

Dark matter. (2007). Wikipedia. Retrieved July 21, 2007, from en.wikipedia.org/wiki/Dark_matter.

de Haas, M. A., Bakermans-Kranenburg, M. J., & van IJzendoorn, M. H. (1994). The Adult Attachment Interview and questionnaires for attachment style, temperament, and memories of parental behavior. *Journal of Genetic Psychology, 155*, 471–86.

De Wolff, M., & van IJzendoorn, M. H. (1997). Sensitivity and attachment: A meta-analysis on parental antecedents of infant attachment. *Child Development, 68*, 571–91.

Diamond, D., Clarkin, J., Levine, H., Levy, K., Foelsch, P., & Yeomans, F. (1999). Borderline conditions and attachment: A preliminary report. *Psychoanalytic Inquiry, 19*, 831–84.

Diamond, D., Clarkin, J. F., Stovall-McClough, K. C., Levy, K. N., Foelsch, P. A., Levine, H., & Yeomans, F. E. (2003). Patient-therapist attachment: Impact on the therapeutic process and outcome. In M. Cortina and M. Marrone (Eds.), *Attachment theory and the psychoanalytic process*. London: Whurr.

Diamond, D., Stovall-McClough, C., Clarkin, J. F., & Levy, K. N. (2003). Patient-therapist attachment in the treatment of borderline personality disorder. *Bulletin of the Menninger Clinic, 67*, 227–59.

Dozier, M. (1990). Attachment organization and treatment use for adults with serious psychopathological disorders. *Development and Psychopathology, 2*, 47–60.

———. (2003). Attachment-based treatment for vulnerable children. *Attachment and Human Development, 5*, 253–57.

Dozier, M., & Bates, B. C. (2004). Attachment state of mind and the treatment relationship. In L. Atkinson and S. Goldberg (Eds.), *Attachment issues in psychopathology and intervention* (pp. 167–80). Mahwah, NJ: Erlbaum.

Dozier, M., Cue, K. L., & Barnett, L. (1994). Clinicians as caregivers: Role of attachment organization in treatment. *Journal of Consulting and Clinical Psychology, 62*, 793–800.

Dozier, M., & Kobak, R. R. (1992). Psychophysiology in attachment: Converging evidence for deactivating strategies. *Child Development, 63*, 1473–80.

Dozier, M., & Lee, S. W. (1995). Discrepancies between self- and other-report of psychiatric symptomatology: Effects of dismissing attachment strategies. *Development and Psychopathology, 7,* 217–26.

Dozier, M., Stevenson, A. L., Lee, S. W., & Velligan, D. I. (1991). Attachment organization and familial overinvolvement for adults with serious psychopathological disorders. *Development and Psychopathology, 3,* 475–89.

Dozier, M., Stovall-McClough, K. C., Albus, K. E., & Bates, B. (2001). Attachment for infants in foster care: The role of caregiver state of mind. *Child Development, 72,* 1467–77.

Dozier, M., & Tyrrell, C. (1998). The role of attachment in therapeutic relationships. In J. A. Simpson and W. S. Rholes (Eds.), *Attachment theory and close relationships* (pp. 221–48). New York: Guilford Press.

Eagle, M. (2003). Clinical implications of attachment theory. *Psychoanalytic Inquiry, 23,* 27–53.

———. (2006). Attachment, psychotherapy, and assessment: A commentary. *Journal of Consulting and Clinical Psychology, 74,* 1086–97.

Eagle, M., & Wolitzky, D. L. (2006, November). *The perspectives of attachment theory and psychoanalysis: Adult psychotherapy.* In M. Eagle and D. L. Wolitzky (Chairs), *The perspectives of attachment theory and psychoanalysis: Adult psychotherapy.* Symposium conducted by Adelphi University and the New York Attachment Consortium, Garden City, New York.

Farber, B. A., & Geller, J. (1994). Gender and representation in psychotherapy. *Psychotherapy, 31,* 318–26.

Farber, B. A., Lippert, R. A., & Nevas, D. B. (1995). The therapist as attachment figure. *Psychotherapy, 32,* 204–12.

Feeney, J. A. (1999). Adult romantic attachment and couple relationships. In J. Cassidy and P. R. Shaver (Eds.), *Handbook of attachment: Theory, research, and clinical applications* (pp. 355–77). New York: Guilford Press.

Ferber, R. (1990). Sleep schedule-dependent causes of insomnia and sleepiness in middle childhood and adolescence. *Pediatrician, 17,* 13–20.

———. (2006). *Solve your child's sleep problems* (Rev. ed.). New York: Fireside.

Ferenczi, S., & Rank, O. (1924). *The development of psychoanalysis.* Madison, CT: International Universities Press.

Flaskerud, J. H. (1990). Matching client and therapist ethnicity, language, and gender: A review of research. *Issues in Mental Health Nursing, 11,* 321–36.

Fonagy, P., Gergely, G., Jurist, E. L., & Target, M. (2002). *Affect regulation, mentalization, and the development of the self.* New York: Other Press.

Fonagy, P., Leigh, T., Steele, M., Steele, H., Kennedy, R., Mattoon, G., Target, M., & Gerber, A. (1996). The relation of attachment status, psychiatric classification, and response to psychotherapy. *Journal of Consulting and Clinical Psychology, 64,* 22–31.

Fonagy, P., Steele, H., & Steele, M. (1991). Maternal representations of attachment during pregnancy predict organization of infant-mother attachment at one year of age. *Child Development, 62,* 891–905.

Fonagy, P., Steele, M., Steele, H., Leigh, T., Kennedy, R., Mattoon, G., & Target, M. (1995). Attachment, the reflective self, and borderline states: The predictive specificity of the Adult Attachment Interview and pathological emotional development. In S. Goldberg, R. Muir, and J. Kerr (Eds.), *Attachment theory: Social, developmental, and clinical perspectives* (pp. 233–78). Hillsdale, NJ: Analytic Press.

Fonagy, P., Target, M., Steele, H., & Steele, M. (1998). *Reflective-functioning manual, version 5: For application to Adult Attachment Interviews*, University College, London.

Fosha, D. (2000). *The transforming power of affect: A model for accelerated change.* New York: Basic Books.

Fraiberg, S., Adelson, E., & Shapiro, V. (1975). Ghosts in the nursery: A psychoanalytic approach to impaired infant-mother relationships. *Journal of the American Academy of Child Psychiatry, 14,* 1387–1422.

Freud, A. (1946). *The psycho-analytical treatment of children.* London: Imago.

Freud, E. L. (Ed.). (1960). *The letters of Sigmund Freud.* New York: Basic Books.

Freud, E. L., Freud, L., & Grubrich-Simitis, I. (Eds.). (1978). *Sigmund Freud: His life in pictures and words.* New York: Harcourt Brace Jovanovich.

Freud, S. (1887–1902). *The origins of psychoanalysis: Letters to Wilhelm Fliess. Drafts and notes: 1887–1902.* In M. Bonaparte, A. Freud, and E. Kris (Eds.), and E. Mosbacher and J. Strachey (Trans.), *The origins of psychoanalyis: Letters to Wilhelm Fliess.* New York: Basic Books, 1954.

———. (1893). Katharina, case histories from studies on hysteria. In J. Strachey (Ed. and Trans.), *The standard edition of the complete psychological works of Sigmund Freud* (Vol. 2, pp. 125–34). London: Hogarth Press, 1955.

———. (1893–1895). Studies on hysteria. In J. Strachey (Ed. and Trans.), *The standard edition of the complete psychological works of Sigmund Freud* (Vol. 2, pp. ix–323). London: Hogarth Press, 1955.

———. (1897). Letter 712 Extracts from the Fliess papers. In J. Strachey (Ed. and Trans.), *The standard edition of the complete psychological works of Sigmund Freud* (Vol. 1, pp. 263–66). London: Hogarth Press, 1966.

———. (1899). Screen memories. In J. Strachey (Ed. and Trans.), *The standard edition of the complete psychological works of Sigmund Freud* (Vol. 3, pp. 303–22). London: Hogarth Press, 1961.

———. (1900). The interpretation of dreams. In J. Strachey (Ed. and Trans.), *The standard edition of the complete psychological works of Sigmund Freud* (Vols. 4 and 5, pp. 1–625). London: Hogarth Press, 1961.

———. (1901). The psychopathology of everyday life. In J. Strachey (Ed. and Trans.), *The standard edition of the complete psychological works of Sigmund Freud* (Vol. 6, pp. vii–296). London: Hogarth Press, 1960.

———. (1905). Three essays on the theory of sexuality. In J. Strachey (Ed. and Trans.), *The standard edition of the complete psychological works of Sigmund Freud* (Vol. 7, pp. 135–243). London: Hogarth Press, 1961.

———. (1906). Letter from Sigmund Freud to C. G. Jung, December 6, 1906. In W. McGuire (Ed. and Trans.), *The Freud/Jung letters: The correspondence between Sigmund Freud and C. G. Jung* (pp. 11–13). Princeton, NJ: Princeton University Press, 1974.

―――. (1909). Notes upon a case of obsessional neurosis. In J. Strachey (Ed. and Trans.), *The standard edition of the complete psychological works of Sigmund Freud* (Vol. 10, pp. 151–318). London: Hogarth Press, 1961.

―――. (1910a). Five lectures on psycho-analysis. In J. Strachey (Ed. and Trans.), *The standard edition of the complete psychological works of Sigmund Freud* (Vol. 11, pp. 1–56). London: Hogarth Press, 1961.

―――. (1910b). The future prospects of psycho-analytic therapy. In J. Strachey (Ed. and Trans.), *The standard edition of the complete psychological works of Sigmund Freud* (Vol. 11, pp. 139–52). London: Hogarth Press, 1961.

―――. (1912a). The dynamics of transference. In J. Strachey (Ed. and Trans.), *The standard edition of the complete psychological works of Sigmund Freud* (Vol. 12, pp. 97–108). London: Hogarth Press, 1961.

―――. (1912b). Recommendations to physicians practising psycho-analysis. In J. Strachey (Ed. and Trans.), *The standard edition of the complete psychological works of Sigmund Freud* (Vol. 12, pp. 109–20). London: Hogarth Press, 1961.

―――. (1913). On beginning the treatment (Further recommendations on the technique of psycho-analysis I). In J. Strachey (Ed. and Trans.), *The standard edition of the complete psychological works of Sigmund Freud* (Vol. 12, pp. 123–44). London: Hogarth Press, 1958.

―――. (1914). Letter from Sigmund Freud to Sándor Ferenczi, June 22, 1914. In E. Brabant, E. Falzeder, and P. Giampieri-Deutsch (Eds. and Trans.), *The correspondence of Sigmund Freud and Sándor Ferenczi* (Vol. 1, pp. 559–60). Cambridge, MA: Belknap Press of Harvard University Press, 1993.

―――. (1915). Observations on transference-love (Further recommendations on the technique of psycho-analysis III). In J. Strachey (Ed. and Trans.), *The standard edition of the complete psychological works of Sigmund Freud* (Vol. 12, pp. 157–71). London: Hogarth Press, 1961.

―――. (1917). A childhood recollection from *Dichtung und Wahrheit*. In J. Strachey (Ed. and Trans.), *The standard edition of the complete psychological works of Sigmund Freud* (Vol. 17, pp. 145–56). London: Hogarth Press, 1955.

―――. (1918). The taboo of virginity (Contributions to the psychology of love III). In J. Strachey (Ed. and Trans.), *The standard edition of the complete psychological works of Sigmund Freud* (Vol. 11, pp. 191–208). London: Hogarth, 1961.

―――. (1919). Lines of advance in psycho-analytic therapy. In J. Strachey (Ed. and Trans.), *The standard edition of the complete psychological works of Sigmund Freud* (Vol. 17, pp. 157–68). London: Hogarth Press, 1955.

―――. (1920). Beyond the pleasure principle. In J. Strachey (Ed. and Trans.), *The standard edition of the complete psychological works of Sigmund Freud* (Vol. 18, pp. 7–64). London: Hogarth Press, 1961.

―――. (1923). The ego and the id. In J. Strachey (Ed. and Trans.), *The standard edition of the complete psychological works of Sigmund Freud* (Vol. 19, pp. 12–66). London: Hogarth Press, 1961.

―――. (1924). The dissolution of the Oedipus complex. In J. Strachey (Ed. and Trans.), *The standard edition of the complete psychological works of Sigmund Freud* (Vol. 19, pp. 171–80). London: Hogarth Press, 1961.

——. (1926). The question of lay analysis: Conversations with an impartial person. In J. Strachey (Ed. and Trans.), *The standard edition of the complete psychological works of Sigmund Freud* (Vol. 20, pp. 183–258). London: Hogarth Press, 1961.

——. (1931). Female sexuality. In J. Strachey (Ed. and Trans.), *The standard edition of the complete psychological works of Sigmund Freud* (Vol. 21, pp. 221–44). London: Hogarth Press, 1961.

——. (1933). New introductory lectures on psycho-analysis. In J. Strachey (Ed. and Trans.), *The standard edition of the complete psychological works of Sigmund Freud* (Vol. 22, pp. 1–182). London: Hogarth Press, 1964.

Gay, P. (1998). *Freud: A life for our time.* New York: W. W. Norton.

George, C., Kaplan, N., & Main, M. (1985). *Adult Attachment Interview.* Unpublished manuscript, University of California, Berkeley.

——. (1996). *Adult Attachment Interview* (Third ed.). Unpublished manuscript, University of California, Berkeley.

George, C., & Solomon, J. (1996). Representational models of relationships: Links between caregiving and attachment. *Infant Mental Health Journal, 17,* 198–216.

——. (1999). Attachment and caregiving: The caregiving behavioral system. In J. Cassidy and P. R. Shaver (Eds.), *Handbook of attachment: Theory, research, and clinical applications* (pp. 649–70). New York: Guilford Press.

George, C., & West, M. (1999). Developmental vs. social personality models of adult attachment and mental ill health. *British Journal of Medical Psychology, 72,* 285–303.

Gergely, G. (2000). Reapproaching Mahler: New perspectives on normal autism, symbiosis, splitting and libidinal object constancy from cognitive developmental theory. *Journal of the American Psychoanalytic Association, 48,* 1197–1228.

Glassman, M. (1988). Kernberg and Kohut: A test of competing psychoanalytic models of narcissism. *Journal of the American Psychoanalytic Association, 36,* 597–625.

Goodman, G. (2002). *The internal world and attachment.* Hillsdale, NJ: The Analytic Press.

——. (2006, November). [Discussant: *The perspectives of attachment theory and psychoanalysis: Adult psychotherapy*]. In M. Eagle & D. L. Wolitzky (Chairs), *The perspectives of attachment theory and psychoanalysis: Adult psychotherapy.* Symposium conducted by Adelphi University and the New York Attachment Consortium, Garden City, New York.

——. (in press-a). *Transforming the Internal World and Attachment: Volume I: Theoretical and Empirical Perspectives.* Lanham, MD: Jason Aronson.

——. (in press-b). *Transforming the Internal World and Attachment: Volume II: Clinical Applications.* Lanham, MD: Jason Aronson.

Goodman, G., Hans, S. L., & Cox, S. M. (1999). Attachment behavior and its antecedents in offspring born to methadone-maintained women. *Journal of Clinical Child Psychology, 28,* 58–69.

Greenberg, J. (2001a). The analyst's participation: A new look. *Journal of the American Psychoanalytic Association, 49,* 359–81.

——. (2001b). The analyst's participation: A new look [Response]. *Journal of the American Psychoanalytic Association, 49,* 417–26.

Greenberg, J. R. (1986). Theoretical models and the analyst's neutrality. *Contemporary Psychoanalysis, 22*, 89–106.

Greenson, R. R. (1965). The working alliance and the transference neurosis. *Psychoanalytic Quarterly, 34*, 155–81.

———. (1967). *The technique and practice of psychoanalysis*. New York: International Universities Press.

Grossmann, K., Grossmann, K. E., Spangler, G., Suess, G., & Unzner, L. (1985). Maternal sensitivity and newborns' orientation responses as related to quality of attachment in northern Germany. In I. Bretherton and E. Waters (Eds.), *Growing points in attachment theory and research. Monographs of the Society for Research in Child Development, 50*(1-2, Serial No. 209), 233–78.

Grossmann, K. E., Grossmann, K., & Waters, E. (Eds.). (2005). *Attachment from infancy to adulthood: The major longitudinal studies*. New York: Guilford Press.

Hamilton, C. E. (2000). Continuity and discontinuity of attachment from infancy through adolescence. *Child Development, 71*, 690–94.

Hardin, H. (1987). On the vicissitudes of Freud's early mothering. I: Early environment and loss. *Psychoanalytic Quarterly, 56*, 628–44.

———. (1988a). On the vicissitudes of Freud's early mothering. II: Alienation from his biological mother. *Psychoanalytic Quarterly, 57*, 72–86.

———. (1988b). On the vicissitudes of Freud's early mothering. III: Freiberg, screen memories, and loss. *Psychoanalytic Quarterly, 57*, 209–24.

Hazan, C., & Shaver, P. R. (1987). Romantic love conceptualized as an attachment process. *Journal of Personality and Social Psychology, 52*, 511–24.

Henry, W. P., & Strupp, H. H. (1994). The therapeutic alliance as interpersonal process. In A. O. Horvath and L. S. Greenberg (Eds.), *The working alliance: Theory, research, and practice* (pp. 51–84). Oxford: Wiley.

Henry, W. P., Strupp, H. H., Butler, S. F., Schacht, T. E., & Binder, J. L. (1993). Effects of training in time-limited dynamic psychotherapy: Changes in therapist behavior. *Journal of Consulting and Clinical Psychology, 61*, 434–40.

Hesse, E. (1996). Discourse, memory, and the Adult Attachment Interview: A note with emphasis on the emerging cannot classify category. *Infant Mental Health Journal, 17*, 4–11.

Hesse, E., & Main, M. (1999). Second-generation effects of unresolved trauma in non maltreating parents: Dissociated, frightened, and threatening parental behavior. *Psychoanalytic Inquiry, 19*, 481–540.

Hindy, C. G., & Schwarz, J. C. (1994). Anxious romantic attachment in adult relationships. In M. B. Sperling and W. H. Berman (Eds.), *Attachment in adults: Clinical and developmental perspectives* (pp. 179–203). New York: Guilford Press.

Hoffman, I. Z. (1994). Dialectical thinking and therapeutic action in the psychoanalytic process. *Psychoanalytic Quarterly, 63*, 187–218.

Hoffman, K. T., Marvin, R. S., Cooper, G., & Powell, B. (2006). Changing toddlers' and preschoolers' attachment classifications: The Circle of Security intervention. *Journal of Consulting and Clinical Psychology, 74*, 1017–26.

Holmes, J. (1996). Psychotherapy and memory: An attachment perspective. *British Journal of Psychotherapy, 13*, 204–18.

———. (1998). The changing aims of psychoanalytic psychotherapy: An integrative perspective. *International Journal of Psycho-Analysis, 79,* 227–40.

Horvath, A., & Greenberg, L. (1989). Development and validation of the Working Alliance Inventory. *Journal of Counseling Psychology, 36,* 223–33.

Horvath, A., & Symonds, B. (1991). Relation between working alliance and outcome in psychotherapy: A meta-analysis. *Journal of Counseling Psychology, 38,* 139–49.

Howes, C. (1999). Attachment relationships in the context of multiple caregivers. In J. Cassidy and P. R. Shaver (Eds.), *Handbook of attachment: Theory, research, and clinical applications* (pp. 671–87). New York: Guilford Press.

Janov, A. (1970). *The primal scream; primal therapy: The cure for neurosis.* New York: Putnam.

Jones, E. (1953). *The life and work of Sigmund Freud: Vol. 1. The formative years and the great discoveries, 1856–1900.* New York: Basic Books.

———. (1955). *Sigmund Freud life and work: Vol. 2. Years of maturity 1901–1919.* New York: Basic Books.

Jones, E. E. (2000). *Therapeutic action: A guide to psychoanalytic therapy.* Northvale, NJ: Jason Aronson.

Kantrowitz, J. (1995). The beneficial aspects of the patient-analyst match. *International Journal of Psycho-Analysis, 76,* 299–313.

———. (2001). The analyst's participation: A new look [Commentary]. *Journal of the American Psychoanalytic Association, 49,* 398–406.

Kernberg, O. (1975). *Borderline conditions and pathological narcissism.* New York: Jason Aronson.

———. (1986a). Borderline personality organization. In M. Stone (Ed.), *Essential papers on borderline disorders: One hundred years at the border* (pp. 279–319). New York: New York University Press.

———. (1986b). Further contributions to the treatment of narcissistic personalities. In A. Morrison (Ed.), *Essential papers on narcissism* (pp. 245–92). New York: New York University Press.

———. (1992). *Aggression in personality disorders and perversions.* New Haven, CT: Yale University Press.

———. (1996). A psychoanalytic theory of personality disorders. In J. F. Clarkin and M. F. Lenzenweger (Eds.), *Major theories of personality disorder* (pp. 106–40). New York: Guilford Press.

Kernberg, O. F., Selzer, M. A., Koenigsberg, H. W., Carr, A. C., & Appelbaum, A. H. (1989). *Psychodynamic psychotherapy of borderline patients.* New York: Basic Books.

Klein, M. (1927). Symposium on child analysis. *International Journal of Psycho-Analysis, 7,* 339–70.

Kobak, R. R., Cole, H. E., Ferenz-Gillies, R., Fleming, W. S., & Gamble, W. (1993). Attachment and emotion regulation during mother-teen problem solving: A control theory analysis. *Child Development, 64,* 231–45.

Kobak, R. R., & Sceery, A. (1988). Attachment in late adolescence: Working models, affect regulation, and representations of self and others. *Child Development, 59,* 135–46.

Kohut, H. (1971). *The analysis of the self: A systematic approach to the psychoanalytic treatment of narcissistic personality disorders.* New York: International Universities Press.

———. (1981, October 4). *Remarks on empathy.* Paper presented at the Conference on Self Psychology, Berkeley, California.

———. (1984). *How does analysis cure?* Chicago: University of Chicago Press.

Lacan, J. (1977). *Écrits: A selection* (A. Sheridan, Trans.). New York: W. W. Norton.

Langs, R. (1976). *The bipersonal field.* New York: Jason Aronson.

Langs, R., & Stone, L. (1980). *The therapeutic experience and its setting: A clinical dialogue.* New York: Jason Aronson.

Levy, K. N. (2005). The implications of attachment theory and research for understanding borderline personality disorder. *Development and Psychopathology, 17,* 959–86.

Linehan, M. M. (1993). *Cognitive-behavioral treatment of borderline personality disorder.* New York: Guilford Press.

Lipton, S. D. (1977). The advantages of Freud's technique as shown in his analysis of the Rat Man. *International Journal of Psycho-Analysis, 58,* 255–73.

Luborsky, L. (1994). Therapeutic alliances as predictors of psychotherapy outcomes: Factors explaining the predictive success. In A. O. Horvath and L. S. Greenberg (Eds.), *The working alliance: Theory, research, and practice* (pp. 38–50). New York: Wiley.

Luborsky, L., Singer, B., & Luborsky, L. (1975). Comparative studies of psychotherapies: Is it true that "everyone has won and all must have prizes"? *Archives of General Psychiatry, 32,* 995–1008.

Lyons, L. S., & Sperling, M. (1996). Clinical applications of attachment theory: Empirical and theoretical perspectives. In J. M. Masling and R. F. Bornstein (Eds.), *Psychoanalytic perspectives on developmental psychology* (pp. 221–56). Washington, DC: American Psychological Association.

Lyons-Ruth, K. (1999). The two-person unconscious: Intersubjective dialogue, enactive relational representation, and the emergence of new forms of relational organization. *Psychoanalytic Inquiry, 19,* 576–617.

Mackie, A. J. (1981). Attachment theory: Its relevance to the therapeutic alliance. *British Journal of Medical Psychology, 54,* 203–12.

Mahler, M. S., Pine, F., & Bergman, A. (1975). *The psychological birth of the human infant: Symbiosis and individuation.* New York: Basic Books.

Main, M., & Goldwyn, R. (1984). Predicting rejection of her infant from mother's representation of her own experience: Implications for the abused-abusing intergenerational cycle. *Child Abuse and Neglect, 8,* 203–17.

———. (1994). *Adult attachment scoring and classification systems* (Sixth ed.). Unpublished manuscript, University College, London.

Main, M., & Hesse, E. (1990). Parents' unresolved traumatic experiences are related to infant disorganized attachment status: Is frightened and/or frightening parental behavior the linking mechanism? In M. T. Greenberg, D. Cicchetti, and E. M.

Cummings (Eds.), *Attachment in the preschool years: Theory, research, and intervention* (pp. 161–82). Chicago: University of Chicago Press.

Main, M., Kaplan, N., & Cassidy, J. (1985). Security in infancy, childhood, and adulthood: A move to the level of representation. In I. Bretherton and E. Waters (Eds.), *Growing points in attachment theory and research. Monographs of the Society for Research in Child Development, 50*(1-2, Serial No. 209), 66–104.

Main, M., & Stadtman, J. (1981). Infant response to rejection of physical contact by the mother: Aggression, avoidance and conflict. *Journal of the American Academy of Child Psychiatry, 20*, 292–307.

Mallinckrodt, B. (2000). Attachment, social competencies, social support, and interpersonal process in psychotherapy. *Psychotherapy Research, 10*, 239–66.

Mallinckrodt, B., Gantt, D. L., & Coble, H. M. (1995). Attachment patterns in the psychotherapy relationship: Development of the Client Attachment to Therapist Scale. *Journal of Counseling Psychology, 42*, 307–17.

Mallinckrodt, B., King, J. L., & Coble, H. M. (1998). Family dysfunction, alexithymia, and client attachment to therapist. *Journal of Counseling Psychology, 45*, 497–504.

Mallinckrodt, B., Porter, M. J., & Kivlighan, D. M., Jr. (2005). Client attachment to therapist, depth of in-session exploration, and object relations in brief psychotherapy. *Psychotherapy: Theory, Research, Practice, Training, 42*, 85–100.

Martin, D. J., Garske, J. P., & Davis, M. K. (2000). Relation of the therapeutic alliance with outcome and other variables: A meta-analytic review. *Journal of Consulting and Clinical Psychology, 68*, 438–50.

Masson, J. M. (Ed. and Trans.). (1985). *The complete letters of Sigmund Freud to Wilhelm Fliess, 1877–1904*. Cambridge, MA: Belknap Press of Harvard University Press.

McBride, C., Atkinson, L., Quilty, L. C., & Bagby, R. M. (2006). Attachment as moderator of treatment outcome in major depression: A randomized control trial of interpersonal psychotherapy versus cognitive behavior therapy. *Journal of Consulting and Clinical Psychology, 74*, 1041–54.

McLaughlin, J. (1991). Clinical and theoretical aspects of enactment. *Journal of the American Psychoanalytic Association, 39*, 595–614.

McWilliams, N. (1999). *Psychoanalytic case formulation*. New York: Guilford Press.

Michels, R. (2001). The analyst's participation: A new look [Commentary]. *Journal of the American Psychoanalytic Association, 49*, 406–10.

Mitchell, S. (1999). Attachment theory and the psychoanalytic tradition: Reflections on human relationality. *Psychoanalytic Dialogues, 9*, 85–107.

Munich, R. L. (1993). Conceptual issues in the psychoanalytic psychotherapy of patients with borderline personality disorder. In W. H. Sledge and A. Tasman (Eds.), *Clinical challenges in psychiatry* (pp. 61–87). Washington, DC: American Psychiatric Press.

Nelson, M. L., & Neufeldt, S. A. (1996). Building on an empirical foundation: Strategies to enhance good practice. *Journal of Counseling and Development, 74*, 609–15.

Ogden, T. H. (1979). On projective identification. *International Journal of Psycho-Analysis, 60,* 357–73.
Parish, M., & Eagle, M. N. (2003). Attachment to the therapist. *Psychoanalytic Psychology, 20,* 271–86.
Pianta, R. C., Egeland, B., & Adam, E. K. (1996). Adult attachment classification and self-reported psychiatric symptomatology as assessed by the Minnesota Multiphasic Personality Inventory-2. *Journal of Consulting and Clinical Psychology, 64,* 273–81.
Reis, B. F., & Brown, L. G. (1999). Reducing psychotherapy dropouts: Maximizing perspective convergence in the psychotherapy dyad. *Psychotherapy, 36,* 123–36.
Rogers, C. R. (1977). *Carl Rogers on personal power.* Oxford: Delacorte Press.
Roisman, G. I., Holland, A., Fortuna, K., Fraley, R. C., Clausell, E., & Clarke, A. (2007). The Adult Attachment Interview and self-reports of attachment style: An empirical rapprochement. *Journal of Personality and Social Psychology, 92,* 678–97.
Roisman, G. I., Tsai, J. L., & Chiang, K.-H. S. (2004). The emotional integration of childhood experience: Physiological, facial expressive, and self-reported emotional response during the Adult Attachment Interview. *Developmental Psychology, 40,* 776–89.
Rosenstein, D. S., & Horowitz, H. A. (1996). Adolescent attachment and psychopathology. *Journal of Consulting and Clinical Psychology, 64,* 244–53.
Safran, J. D., & Muran, J. C. (2000). *Negotiating the therapeutic alliance: A relational treatment guide.* New York: Guilford Press.
Sandler, J. (1960). The background of safety. *International Journal of Psycho-Analysis, 41,* 352–56.
Schafer, R. (1983). *The analytic attitude.* New York: Basic Books.
Schore, A. N. (2003). *Affect regulation and the repair of the self.* New York: W. W. Norton.
Shedler, J., Mayman, M., & Manis, M. (1993). The illusion of mental health. *American Psychologist, 48,* 1117–31.
———. (1994). More illusions. *American Psychologist, 49,* 974–76.
Simpson, J. A. (1990). Influence of attachment styles on romantic relationships. *Journal of Personality and Social Psychology, 59,* 971–80.
Skinner, B. F. (1974). *About behaviorism.* New York: Vintage Books.
Slade, A. (1999). Attachment theory and research: Implications for the theory and practice of individual psychotherapy with adults. In J. Cassidy and P. R. Shaver (Eds.), *Handbook of attachment: Theory, research, and clinical applications* (pp. 575–94). New York: Guilford Press.
Smallbone, S. W., & Dodds, M. R. (2001). Further evidence for a relationship between attachment insecurity and coercive sexual behavior in nonoffenders. *Journal of Interpersonal Violence, 16,* 22–35.
Solomon, J., & George, C. (1999). The place of disorganization in attachment theory: Linking classic observations with contemporary findings. In J. Solomon and C. George (Eds.), *Attachment disorganization* (pp. 3–32). New York: Guilford Press.

Spangler, G., & Grossmann, K. E. (1993). Biobehavioral organization in securely and insecurely attached infants. *Child Development, 64,* 1439–50.

Sperling, M. B., & Berman, W. H. (1991). An attachment classification of desperate love. *Journal of Personality Assessment, 56,* 45–55.

Sperling, M. B., Foelsch, P., & Grace, C. (1996). Measuring adult attachment: Are self-report instruments congruent? *Journal of Personality Assessment, 67,* 37–51.

Sroufe, L. A., & Waters, E. (1977). Heart rate as a convergent measure in clinical and developmental research. *Merrill-Palmer Quarterly, 23,* 3–27.

Stern, D. N. (1977). *The first relationship: Mother and infant.* Cambridge, MA: Harvard University Press.

———. (1985). *The interpersonal world of the infant: A view from psychoanalysis and developmental psychology.* New York: Basic Books.

———. (1995). *The motherhood constellation: A unified view of parent-infant psychotherapy.* New York: Basic Books.

Stern, D. N., Sander, L. W., Nahum, J. P., Harrison, A. M., Lyons-Ruth, K., Morgan, A. C., Bruschweiler-Stern, N., & Tronick, E. Z. (1998). Non-interpretive mechanisms in psychoanalytic therapy: The "something more" than interpretation. *International Journal of Psycho-Analysis, 79,* 903–21.

Szajnberg, N. M., & Crittenden, P. M. (1997). The transference refracted through the lens of attachment. *Journal of the American Academy of Psychoanalysis, 25,* 409–38.

Talley, P. F., Strupp, H. H., & Morey, L. C. (1990). Match-making in psychotherapy: Patient-therapist dimensions and their impact on outcome. *Journal of Consulting and Clinical Psychology, 58,* 182–88.

Tracey, T. J. (1987). Stage differences in the dependencies of topic initiation and topic following behavior. *Journal of Counseling Psychology, 34,* 123–31.

Tracey, T. J., & Ray, P. B. (1984). Stages of successful time-limited counseling: An interactional examination. *Journal of Counseling Psychology, 31,* 13–27.

Treurniet, N. (1993). What is psychoanalysis now? *International Journal of Psycho-Analysis, 74,* 873–91.

Tronick, E. Z., Bruschweiler-Stern, N., Harrison, A. M., Lyons-Ruth, K., Morgan, A. C., Nahum, J. P., Sander, L., & Stern, D. N. (1998). Dyadically expanded states of consciousness and the process of therapeutic change. *Infant Mental Health Journal, 19,* 290–99.

Tyrrell, C. L., Dozier, M., Teague, G. B., & Fallot, R. D. (1999). Effective treatment relationships for persons with serious psychiatric disorders: The importance of attachment states of mind. *Journal of Consulting and Clinical Psychology, 67,* 725–33.

van IJzendoorn, M. H. (1995). Adult attachment representations, parental responsiveness, and infant attachment: A meta-analysis on the predictive validity of the Adult Attachment Interview. *Psychological Bulletin, 117,* 387–403.

Vitz, P. C. (1977). *Psychology as religion: The cult of self-worship.* Grand Rapids, MI: William B. Eerdmans.

Vygotsky, L. (1978). *Mind in society: The development of higher psychological processes.* Cambridge, MA: Harvard University Press.

Wampold, B. E. (2001). *The great psychotherapy debate: Models, methods, and findings.* Mahwah, NJ: Erlbaum.
Waters, E., Merrick, S., Treboux, D., Crowell, J., & Albersheim, L. (2000). Attachment security in infancy and early adulthood: A twenty-year longitudinal study. *Child Development, 71,* 684–89.
Watson, J. B. (1928). *Psychological care of infant and child.* New York: W. W. Norton.
Weiss, J., & Sampson, H. (1986). *The psychoanalytic process: Theory, clinical observation, and empirical research.* New York: Guilford Press.
West, M., Sheldon, A., & Reiffer, L. (1987). An approach to the delineation of adult attachment: Scale development and reliability. *Journal of Nervous and Mental Disease, 175,* 738–41.
Westen, D., & Gabbard, G. O. (2002). Developments in cognitive neuroscience: II. Implications for theories of transference. *Journal of the American Psychoanalytic Association, 50,* 99–134.
Westen, D., Nakash, O., Thomas, C., & Bradley, R. (2006). Clinical assessment of attachment patterns and personality disorder in adolescents and adults. *Journal of Consulting and Clinical Psychology, 74,* 1065–85.
Winnicott, D. W. (1960). The theory of the parent-infant relationship. *International Journal of Psycho-Analysis, 41,* 585–95.
———. (1965). *The maturational processes and the facilitating environment: Studies in the theory of emotional development.* New York: International Universities Press.
———. (1971). *Playing and reality.* New York: Basic Books.
Woodhouse, S. S., Schlosser, L. Z., Crook, R. E., Ligiero, D. P., & Gelso, C. J. (2003). Client attachment to therapist: Relations to transference and client recollections of parental caregiving. *Journal of Counseling Psychology, 50,* 395–408.
Yeomans, F. E., Selzer, M. A., & Clarkin, J. F. (1992). *Treating the borderline patient: A contract-based approach.* New York: Basic Books.
Zeanah, C. H., & Smyke, A. T. (2005). Building attachment relationships following maltreatment and severe deprivation. In L. J. Berlin, Y. Ziv, L. Amaya-Jackson, and M. T. Greenberg (Eds.), *Enhancing early attachments: Theory, research, intervention, and policy* (pp. 195–216). New York: Guilford Press.
Zetzel, E. R. (1956). Current concepts of transference. *International Journal of Psycho-Analysis, 37,* 369–75.

Author Index

Abraham, K., 14
Adam, E. K., 73
Adelson, E., 58
Ainsworth, M. D. S., 11, 36, 73, 80
Albersheim, L., 40
Albus, K. E., 19, 35, 71
Alexander, F., 3, 20, 25, 32, 47, 50, 57, 99
Allen, J. G., 94–97
Allen, J. P., 81
Altman, N., 35
Amini, F., 25
Appelbaum, A. H., 18, 39, 41, 52, 61, 65, 83
Arizmendi, T. G., 47
Arnarson, E. O., 1
Aron, L., 34, 35, 63, 96, 98
Atkinson, L., 53, 54, 57, 94

Bagby, R. M., 53, 54, 57, 94
Bakermans-Kranenburg, M. J., 73
Barnett, L., 15, 16, 19, 47, 48, 50, 58, 59, 91, 93, 99
Bartholomew, K., 73
Bates, B. C., 2, 15, 16, 19, 31, 35, 47, 51, 53, 59, 71, 91, 93, 99
Baumbacher, G., 25
Beck, A. T., 51
Bell, S. M., 36

Benjamin, J., 29, 33
Bergan, J., 47
Bergman, A., 24, 26
Berman, W. H., 73
Bernier, A., 15–16, 19, 25, 47, 50, 59, 91, 93, 99
Berzins, J. I., 47
Beutler, L. E., 47
Binder, J. L., 56
Bion, W. R., 34, 58, 60, 61, 87, 88, 97
Bjornsson, A. S., 1
Blehar, M. C., 11, 73, 80
Bordin, E. S., 27, 37, 42
Borman-Spurrell, E., 81
Bowlby, J., 1, 9, 23–26, 29, 30, 39, 45, 49, 69–71
Bradley, R., 27, 37, 40, 73
Brennan, K. A., 73
Briggs, R., 35
Britton, R., 61
Brown, L. G., 47
Bruschweiler-Stern, N., 31–32, 64, 66
Burns, P., 26
Butler, S. F., 56

Carr, A. C., 18, 39, 41, 52, 61, 65, 83
Casement, P. J., 19, 58, 66, 98
Cassidy, J., 14, 30, 46, 70, 73, 80
Charone, J. K., 47

Chiang, K.-H. S., 81
Clark, C. L., 73
Clark, R. W., 12
Clarke, A., 50, 73
Clarkin, J. F., 4, 25, 37, 47, 48, 50, 52, 72–74, 81–89, 92
Clausell, E., 50, 73
Coble, H. M., 4, 25, 74–77, 79
Cole, H. E., 10, 14, 16, 47, 49, 92, 99
Collins, N. L., 73
Cooper, G., 46, 49, 96, 98
Cox, S. M., 74
Crago, M., 47
Craighead, W. E., 1
Crastnopol, M., 46
Crittenden, P. M., 37, 51, 56
Crook, R. E., 40, 78
Crowell, J. A., 40, 73
Cue, K. L., 15, 16, 19, 47, 48, 50, 58, 59, 91, 93, 99
Curhan, J. R., 20

Davis, M. K., 27
de Haas, M. A., 73
De Wolff, M., 46
Diamond, D., 4, 25, 37, 48, 50, 72–74, 81–89, 92
Dodds, M. R., 74
Dozier, M., 2, 15–16, 19, 25, 31–32, 35, 38, 47–51, 53, 55, 57–59, 70–71, 73, 81, 84, 91–93, 99

Eagle, M. N., 4, 20, 25, 27, 33, 37, 45, 46, 49, 54, 57, 61, 62, 72–73, 79, 94
Egeland, B., 73

Fallot, R. D., 15, 19, 38, 47, 49, 50, 59, 84, 92, 93, 99
Farber, B. A., 25, 28, 29
Feeney, J. A., 76
Ferber, R., 28
Ferenczi, S., 20
Ferenz-Gillies, R., 10, 14, 16, 47, 49, 92, 99

Flaskerud, J. H., 47
Fleming, W. S., 10, 14, 16, 47, 49, 92, 99
Foelsch, P. A., 4, 25, 37, 48, 50, 73–74, 81, 83
Fonagy, P., 33, 35, 59, 61, 74, 82, 86, 95
Fortuna, K., 50, 73
Fosha, D., 51
Fraiberg, S., 58
Fraley, R. C., 50, 73
Frankel, J., 35
French, T. M., 3, 20, 25, 32, 47, 50, 57, 99
Freud, A., 35
Freud, E. L., 12, 13
Freud, L., 12
Freud, S., 1, 2, 7–14, 16, 19–21, 24, 26–27, 32, 37, 38–39, 51, 56, 91

Gabbard, G. O., 27
Gamble, W., 10, 14, 16, 47, 49, 92, 99
Gantt, D. L., 4, 25, 74–77, 79
Garske, J. P., 27
Gay, P., 14, 15, 17
Geller, J., 29
Gelso, C. J., 40, 78
Gensler, D., 35
George, C., 12, 34, 41–42, 64, 73, 88–89
Gerber, A., 86
Gergely, G., 33, 59–61, 86, 95
Glassman, M., 51–52
Goldwyn, R., 11, 12, 14, 16, 38, 73, 81, 83, 86, 92
Goodman, G., 5, 16, 19, 28, 31, 40, 41, 48, 52, 55, 62, 66, 74, 81
Grace, C., 73
Greenberg, J. R., 17–19, 26, 27, 55, 92
Greenberg, L., 27, 37, 69
Greenson, R. R., 14, 26, 27
Grossmann, K. E., 17, 39, 81
Grubrich-Simits, I., 12

Author Index

Hagaman, R., 47
Hamilton, C. E., 39
Hans, S. L., 74
Hardin, H., 10, 12
Harrison, A. M., 31–32, 64, 66
Hauser, S. T., 81
Hazan, C., 73
Heim, A. K., 27, 37
Henry, W. P., 36, 56
Hesse, E., 86
Hindy, C. G., 73
Hoffman, I. Z., 17, 92
Hoffman, K. T., 46, 49, 92, 98
Holland, A., 50, 73
Holmes, J., 25
Horowitz, H. A., 81
Horowitz, L. M., 73
Horvath, A., 27, 37, 69
Howes, C., 35

Janov, A., 51
Jobe, A. M., 47
Jones, E., 10, 13
Jones, E. E., 18, 46
Julia, H., 26
Jurist, E. L., 33, 59, 61, 86, 95

Kantrowitz, J. L., 18, 46, 92
Kaplan, N., 12, 30, 34, 70, 73, 80
Kennedy, R., 86
Kernberg, O. F., 18, 39–41, 51, 52, 58, 61, 65, 81, 83
King, J. L., 4, 25, 74, 77
Kivilighan, D. M., Jr., 4, 25, 36, 72, 74, 77, 78, 94–97
Klein, M., 35
Kobak, R. R., 10, 14, 16, 47, 49, 73, 81, 92, 99
Koenigsberg, H. W., 18, 39, 41, 52, 61, 65, 83
Kohut, H., 3, 39, 51, 52

Lacan, J., 32
Langs, R., 58, 64
Lannon, R., 25

Larose, S., 15, 16, 19, 47, 50, 59, 91, 93, 99
Lee, S. W., 73
Leigh, T., 86
Levine, H., 4, 25, 37, 48, 50, 73–74, 81, 83
Levy, K. N., 4, 25, 37, 48, 50, 70, 72–74, 81–89, 92
Lewis, T., 25
Ligiero, D. P., 40, 78
Linehan, M. M., 65
Lippert, R. A., 25, 28
Lipton, S. D., 7
Louie, A., 25
Luborsky, L., 27, 47
Lyons, L. S., 25
Lyons-Ruth, K., 24, 31–35, 37, 42–43, 61–66

Mackie, A. J., 25, 26, 36
Mahler, M. S., 24, 26
Main, M., 11–12, 14, 16, 30, 34, 38, 70, 73, 80, 81, 83, 86, 92
Mallinckrodt, B., 4, 25, 36, 72, 74–79, 94–97
Manis, M., 73
Martin, D. J., 27
Marvin, R. S., 46, 49, 96, 98
Masson, J. M., 14
Mattoon, G., 86
Mayman, M., 73
McBride, C., 53, 54, 57, 94
McGuinness, T., 25
McLaughlin, J. T., 32, 62
McWilliams, N., 30
Merrick, S., 40
Michels, R., 17
Mitchell, S. A., 25
Morey, L. C., 47
Morgan, A. C., 31–32, 64, 66
Munich, R. L., 52
Muran, J. C., 27

Nahum, J. P., 31–32, 64, 66
Nakash, O., 40, 73

Nelson, M. L., 47
Neufeldt, S. A., 47
Nevas, D. B., 25, 28

Ogden, T. H., 61

Pantone, P., 35
Parish, M., 4, 25, 27, 37, 45, 72, 73, 79
Pentland, A., 20
Pianta, R. C., 73
Pine, F., 24, 26
Pollack, S., 47
Porter, M. J., 4, 25, 36, 72, 74, 77, 78, 94–97
Powell, B., 46, 49, 96, 98

Quilty, L. C., 53, 54, 57, 94

Rank, O., 20
Ray, P. B., 52
Read, S. J., 73
Reiffer, L., 73
Reis, B. F., 47
Rodenberg, M., 46
Rogers, C. R., 24
Roisman, G. I., 50, 73, 81
Rosenstein, D. S., 81

Safran, J. D., 27
Sampson, H., 25, 67
Sander, L. W., 26, 31–32, 64, 66
Sandler, J., 25
Sceery, A., 73
Schacht, T. E., 56
Schafer, R., 25
Schiff, E. Z., 25
Schlosser, L. Z., 40, 78
Schore, A. N., 35
Schwarz, J. C., 73
Selzer, M. A., 18, 39, 41, 52, 61, 65, 83
Shanfield, S., 47
Shapiro, V., 58
Shaver, P. R., 73
Shedler, J., 73

Sheets, E. S., 1
Sheldon, A., 73
Simpson, J. A., 73
Singer, B., 47
Skinner, B. F., 51
Slade, A., 37, 56, 70, 92
Smallbone, S. W., 74
Smyke, A. T., 73
Solomon, J., 41–42, 64, 88–89
Soucy, N., 15, 16, 19, 47, 50, 59, 91, 93, 99
Spangler, G., 17, 81
Sperling, M. B., 25, 73
Sroufe, L. A., 81
Stadtman, J., 11
Stayton, D. J., 35
Stone, L., 58, 64
Stechler, G., 26
Steele, H., 74, 82, 86
Steele, M., 74, 82, 86
Stern, D. N., 24, 31–32, 64, 66, 70
Stevenson, A. L., 73
Stovall-McClough, K. C., 4, 19, 25, 35, 37, 48, 50, 71, 72, 74, 81–89, 92
Strupp, H. H., 36, 47, 56
Suess, G., 17
Symonds, B., 27
Szajnberg, N. M., 37, 51, 56

Talley, P. F., 47
Target, M., 33, 59, 61, 82, 86, 95
Teague, G. B., 15, 19, 38, 47, 49, 50, 59, 84, 92, 93, 99
Thomas, C., 40, 73
Tracey, T. J., 52
Treboux, D., 40, 73
Treurniet, N., 20
Tronick, E. Z., 31–32, 64, 66
Tsai, J. L., 81
Tyrrell, C., 15, 16, 19, 31–32, 38, 47, 49–51, 53, 55, 57, 59, 70–71, 84, 91–93, 99

Unzner, L., 17

van IJzendoorn, M. H., 40, 46, 70, 73
Velligan, D. I., 73
Vitz, P. C., 24
Vygotsky, L. S., 19, 87

Wall, S., 11, 73, 80
Wampold, B. E., 5
Waters, E., 11, 39, 40, 73, 80, 81
Watson, J. B., 14–15
Weiss, J., 25, 67
West, M., 73

Westen, D., 27, 37, 40, 73
Winnicott, D. W., 24, 55, 66, 94, 96, 98
Wolitzky, D. L., 33, 61, 62
Woodhouse, S. S., 40, 46, 78

Yeomans, F. E., 4, 25, 37, 48, 50, 52, 73–74, 81, 83

Zeanah, C. H., 73
Zetzel, E. R., 19, 27

Subject Index

abstinence, 19
  Freud on, 8, 15, 21
Adult Attachment Interview (AAI), 34, 38, 73, 74, 76
  See also Patient-Therapist Adult Attachment Interview
affect regulation, 16–17, 21, 31, 34, 49–53
  See also secondary attachment strategies, interaction between therapist and patient's
alpha function, 61
Asperger's disorder, 97
attachment
  internal working models of, 37
  length of time it takes to form, 71–73
  nature of, 39
  parenting behavior and, 46
  to therapist, *39*
    attachment history of therapist and, 69–70
    empirical approaches to assessing, 74–89
    problem of, 36
  validity of self-report measures of adult, 73–74
  See also specific topics
Attachment Q-Set (AQS), 47–48

attachment relationships, development of, 35–36
attachment system of patient and caregiving system of therapist, 41–42, 88–89
attacks on linking, 87
availability (caregiver-infant relationship), 26

bond between patient and therapist, 27
borderline personality disorder (BPD) and borderline personality organization, 39, 40, 49, 52, 60, 83, 98
boundaries, 28–29, 94–97
  See also treatment frame

caregiver-infant attachment relationship
  contrasted with therapist-patient relationship, 23–24, 27–32, 43, 70
  facets of, 25
  as metaphor for therapist-patient relationship, 23, 34, 35, 43, 54, 59, 70–71
caregiver sensitivity and attachment organization, 46
caregiving system of therapist and attachment system of patient, *39*, 41–42, 88–89
case management, 47–49, 84

125

change, first *vs.* second order, 33, 61, 62
chaotic interaction structure, *93*, 95–96
Client Attachment to Therapist Scale (CATS), 75–79
"coasting," 94
cognitive-behavioral therapy (CBT)
   attachment patterns and, 53, 54
   for avoidant patients, 54
   for depression, 53, 94
complementary interactions
   needed early in treatment, 52–54
   when patients need noncomplementary *vs.*, 56–58
   See also secondary attachment strategies
Components of Attachment Questionnaire (CAQ), 79–81
containing interaction structure, *93*, 97–98
containment, 31, 60–61
   See also treatment frame
corrective emotional experience, 57, 59, 92
   noncomplementarity and, 18–21, 25, 47, 50, 54–55, 57, 99
   See also therapist(s), must be experienced as old and new object
couch, use of, 9

deactivating attachment system, 16
   See also secondary attachment strategies
deactivating patient and hyperactivating therapist (expressive interaction structure), *93*, 96–97
deactivating therapist and hyperactivating patient (containing interaction structure), *93*, 97–98
deactivating therapist and patient (sterile interaction structure), *93*, 94–95
depression, 53, 94
dismissing attachment relationship, 12
   AAI and, 14
   Kobak on, 14, 16
   See also specific topics

dismissing features, therapists with, 19
   See also Freud, Sigmund; Watson, John B.
dismissing persons, characteristics of, 14

emotional coldness in analyst, 8
empathic emotion-reflective interactions, 60–61
empathic stance of Kohut, 51–52
enactive procedural representations, 34
enactments, 32, 33, 62–64
expectations, developing new, 31
Experiences of Close Relationships Scale (ECRS), 77–78
expressive interaction structure, *93*, 96–97

financial factors and therapist-patient relationship, 30, 59–60, 62–64
first order change, 33, 62
foster care, 31–32, 36, 66–67, 70–71
Freud, Sigmund
   on analyst-patient relationship, 21, 24
   cure "effected by love," 15–17
   on mother-infant relationship, 9–10, 13
   overregulated affect in, 16–17
   relationship with his mother, 10–13
      dismissing attachment relationship, 10–14, 17
   technical recommendations of, 7–8, 17, 20
      cultural origins of, 17
      intrapsychic origins of, 10–15
      patient population and, 15–17
      representational model and, 8, 15
      theoretical changes and, 7

gender of therapist, 29
"gentle challenge," 3, 19, 53, 59, 96, 97
goals of treatment, 27, 57
grandiose self, 40

"heavy going," 95
histrionic personality, 16

holding environment. *See* containment; treatment frame
hyperactivating patient and deactivating therapist (containing interaction structure), *93*, 97–98
hyperactivating/preoccupied attachment strategy
   academic mentoring relationships and, 50
   borderline personality organization and, 40, 41
   case managers and, 47–49, 84
   characteristics of, 16
   Freud's technical recommendations and, 20
   See also secondary attachment strategies
hyperactivating therapist and deactivating patient (expressive interaction structure), *93*, 96–97
hyperactivating therapist and patient (chaotic interaction structure), *93*, 95–96
hysteria, patients with, 15–17

implicit procedural knowledge
   challenging patient's, 54
   classical psychoanalysis and, 32
   compared with dark matter, 63–66
   detecting, 64
   enactments and, 32
   internal working models and, 37, 43
   language and, 35, 43
   therapeutic change and, 32, 33, 35, 50, 57, 61–66, 72, 99
implicit relational knowledge, 64
   therapeutic change and, 33
independence, parental emphasis on, 17
internal working models, 37, 40–41, 43
interpersonal therapy (IPT) for depression, 53

Kleinians *vs.* Freudians, 35
K-link (Bion), 61

language, acquisition and use of, 32–35, 43

marking, 33–34, 59–62, 95, 96, 98
mentalization, 19
   See also reflective functioning
mentalizing, therapist's private, 88
mental organization in patients *vs.* infants, 30–31
mental representation (caregiver-infant relationship), 26
money and therapist-patient relationship, 30, 59–60, 62–64

narcissistic *vs.* borderline personality, 40–41, 51–52
negative transference, 26, 42
neutrality, 18, 19
   Freud on, 8, 15
noncomplementarity, therapeutic principle of
   attachment security and, 48–49
   attachment styles/strategies and, 16, 19, 20, 47–48
   caregiver-infant relationship and, 23
   case managers and, 47–49, 84
   Freud's technical recommendations and, 16, 20
   phases of treatment and, 52–54, 56–57
   treatment outcome research and, 47–51
   See also secondary attachment strategies; therapist-patient mismatching and successful outcomes
noncomplementary stance of therapist, patient's complying with *vs.* responding authentically, 57–58
noncomplementary states of mind and working alliance, 38
nonsymbolic knowledge, 33
   See also presymbolic communication and knowledge
nonsymbolic mental processing, 35

nonverbal relationship between therapist and patient, 20, 21

Oedipus complex, 29
  Freud and, 9, 10
overregulated therapeutic technique, 16–17

particularity (caregiver-infant relationship), 26
pathways model of therapeutic relationship, *39*, 40–42, 88–89
Patient-Therapist Adult Attachment Interview (PT-AAI), 4, 81–89
personality organization/internal working model, 40–41
  See also internal working models
positive transference, 26
  unobjectionable, 26–27
"positive wrap-up," 12
preoccupied attachment strategy.
  See hyperactivating/preoccupied attachment strategy
presymbolic communication and knowledge, 32
  See also nonsymbolic knowledge; symbolic *vs.* relational procedural knowledge
primary mode of relatedness, 56, 70
projective identification, 61
proximity seeking, 25

race of therapist, 29–30
reflective functioning (RF), 4, 82, 84–89
  See also mentalization
relatedness, primary mode of, 56, 70
relational procedural knowledge. *See* symbolic *vs.* relational procedural knowledge
Relationship Questionnaire (RQ), 80
reverie, 88
rhythmic third, 33

safe haven, 25, 26
safety in analytic situation
  balance between danger and, 55
  See also secure base
secondary attachment strategies, 91–92
  challenging patients', 57
  and complementary *vs.* noncomplementary behavior, 56, 84
  interaction between therapist and patient's, 15–16, 29, 47–49, 84, 91, 92. *See also specific interaction structures*
  interaction structures, 92–99, *93*
  therapists need to know about their, 56
  and treatment modalities and outcomes, 51–55
second order change, 33, 61
secure base, 37
  and experiencing therapist as insecure base, 55
  nature of, 25
  psychoanalytic concepts similar to, 25
secure base provision, 25, 45, 46
  defined, 46
self psychology, 40–41
  See also empathic stance of Kohut
self-reliance, parental emphasis on, 17
separation from therapist, 64–65
separation protest, 25
"smooth sailing," 96, 97
sterile interaction structure, *93*, 94–95
stronger/wiser (caregiver-infant relationship), 25–26
strong feelings (caregiver-infant relationship), 26
structural *vs.* topographic model, and technique, 7
symbolic *vs.* relational procedural knowledge, 32–33, 42, 61–62

Tausk, Victor, 14
technical recommendations
  dialectic of distinctive and flexible, 17–20
  See also Freud, Sigmund

technical taboos, 18
therapeutic alliance, 27
   PT-AAI as measure of, 88
   See also working alliance
therapist-patient matching, 47
   attachment styles and, 15–16, 19, 46. *See also* noncomplementarity
therapist-patient mismatching and successful outcomes, 47
   See also noncomplementarity
therapist-patient relationship
   facets of, 25
   factors that influence, 28–30
   metaphors for, 24–25. *See also* caregiver-infant attachment relationship
   parameters of, 28–29
   pathways model of, 39, 40–42, 88–89
   See also specific topics
therapist(s)
   attachment styles of, 16, 19, 42, 56
   availability during emergencies, 65
   characteristics of, 29–30, 47
   expectations of patient behavior, 31
   must be experienced as old and new object, 18–19, 56–59. *See also* corrective emotional experience
   primary task of
      Bowlby on, 25
      Winniccott on, 55
   vacations of, 64
   when to behave in complementary *vs.* noncomplementary manner, 56–58
time-limited therapies. *See* treatment, length of
transference, 38–39
   vs. attachment, 35–36, 38–40
   attachment to therapist as providing context for, 40
   definitions of, 37, 38
   Freud on, 26–27
   maximizing patient's opportunity to develop, 19–20
   PT-AAI as measure of, 88
   types and components of, 26–27, 39
   See also therapist(s), must be experienced as old and new object
transference-countertransference paradigms, 39, 41–43
Transforming the Internal World and Attachment (Goodman), 5
"transmission gap" (between caregiver sensitivity and attachment), 46
treatment
   goals of, 27, 57
   length of, 57, 72–73
   phases of, 52–54, 56–57
treatment frame, 52, 58, 64
treatment modalities as hyperactivating *vs.* deactivating, 51–52
treatment outcomes
   research on, 47–51
   treatment modality, secondary attachment strategies, and, 51–55

Watson, John B.
   dismissing attitude toward parenting, 14–15
working alliance, 26, 27, 38
   attachment and, 36–38, 39
   noncomplementary stance and, 52–53
   See also therapeutic alliance
Working Alliance Inventory (WAI), 27, 76, 78

zone of proximal development, 19, 87

About the Author

Geoff Goodman, PhD, is associate professor of psychology at Long Island University. He is also a licensed clinical and school psychologist with a private practice in Manhattan and New City and is certified by the American Board of Professional Psychology (ABPP). Goodman earned a PhD in clinical psychology from Northwestern University, and he completed a child clinical psychology internship at Babies Hospital, Columbia-Presbyterian Medical Center, a two-year postdoctoral fellowship in developmental research at Columbia University under Larry Aber, and a two-year postdoctoral fellowship in the research and treatment of borderline personality disorder under Frank Yeomans and Otto Kernberg.

Goodman was instructor of psychology in psychiatry at Cornell University Medical College from 1995 to 1998 and was assistant unit chief of the children's psychiatric inpatient unit. He also holds adjunct faculty positions at Columbia University and Weill Medical College of Cornell University, and he is an advanced candidate in the child and adult programs at the Psychoanalytic Training Institute of the New York Freudian Society. Goodman is the author of over a dozen articles on the development of psychopathology in high-risk infants, children, and adults and of *The Internal World and Attachment* (2002).

Breinigsville, PA USA
06 December 2009
228697BV00004B/1/P